Tell My Peop[le]

Clifford Hill is widely [...] prophet. Academically he [is both a sociologist and a] theologian. He was ordained into the Congregational Church and was National President in 1976/7. He has held two London pastorates and has preached and lectured extensively both in Britain and in the USA.

Dr Hill is known internationally for his writing and broadcast work in race relations. He is used as a consultant by the Home Office, the Police and the Prison Service on the issues of race, culture and violence in society and the problems of the inner city. He has had personal experience of living and working in a multi-racial community in the East End of London, where he founded the Newham Community Renewal Programme. He was also a co-founder of the Martin Luther King Foundation. He has been a senior lecturer in Sociology in the University of London, specializing in the Sociology of Religion, and a part-time lecturer at Spurgeon's Theological College, as well as an examiner in Divinity of the University of London Institute of Education. His degrees include M.A., B.D. and Ph.D. (Theol.).

After leaving the East End Dr Hill gave a period of service as national director of evangelism for the Evangelical Alliance. Since 1981 he has been exercising an international ministry.

First published in 1983 by Fount Paperbacks, London
Third Impression May 1985

© Clifford Hill 1983

Made and printed in Great Britain by
William Collins Sons & Co. Ltd, Glasgow

*By the same author
available as Fount Paperbacks*

TOWARDS THE DAWN
What's Going to Happen to Britain?

THE DAY COMES
A Prophetic View of the Contemporary World

BIBLE REFERENCES

Unless otherwise noted, all Bible references are taken
from the Holy Bible, New International Version,
Copyright © 1978 by New York International Bible
Society. First published in Great Britain in 1979. Used
by permission of New York International Bible
Society.

CLIFFORD HILL

Tell My People
I Love Them

*

FOR GOD SO LOVED THE WORLD THAT HE
GAVE HIS ONE AND ONLY SON, THAT
WHOEVER BELIEVES IN HIM SHALL NOT
PERISH BUT HAVE ETERNAL LIFE.

JOHN 3:16 AND 17

Collins
FOUNT PAPERBACKS

Contents

Foreword

Those who are familiar with Dr Clifford Hill's earlier books *Towards the Dawn* and *The Day Comes* will find this rather different. His basic suppositions are the same but this book is written at a much more popular level. It is a 'Tract for the Times'. Clifford Hill is a man with a burden comparable with that of Jeremiah. He is not a 'prophet of doom' although he does not mince matters when describing the dangers facing the world today. He longs to see men and nations pulling back from otherwise inevitable disaster.

Knowing Clifford as I do, I recognize the personal cost involved in writing this book. He lays bare his soul. Clifford tells us of the spiritual pilgrimage which brought him from a rather arid academic approach to Christianity into a personal dynamic faith in the living Christ. It is particularly moving to read of how God spoke to him through a dramatic incident he witnessed in the Swiss Alps.

It is not easy to single out any particular section of this book. There is a balance between stern warning and earnest entreaty. Preachers will particularly delight in Clifford Hill's treatment of such Old Testament characters as the prophet Jeremiah and King Hezekiah. He clearly feels a kinship with them.

It is little short of a miracle that a man who started his ministry steeped in liberal theology should come to write a book of this kind which is biblically-based throughout. The explanation lies in the fact that Clifford was greatly influenced by the renewal movement some years after he was ordained and he has, amongst other spiritual gifts, exercised a prophetic ministry. He is a man who feels deeply and the title of the book sums up the message he believes people need to hear. The God who sits in judgement over a rebellious world nevertheless is longsuffering and compassionate, not willing that any should perish.

The Rev. Gilbert W. Kirby MA

Preface

This book is different from anything I have written before. Although part of a series that began with the publication of *Towards the Dawn*, it is much simpler and more direct in its message. Essentially it is a book of personal witness.

Only those who know me intimately can be aware of the cost of writing this book. Personal testimony does not come easily to me. I was not brought up in that tradition. Moreover, I received a highly academic and liberal education in both sociology and theology, each of which I pursued to doctoral level. For years I have *thought* as an academic and a sociologist, analysing each situation and belief-system in terms of its social attributes and derivations.

The coming of the Holy Spirit into my life made a revolutionary impact. It caused me to rethink even my most basic and fundamental presuppositions. My rationality demanded that an answer be found to cope with the reality of a personal encounter with God that could not be accounted for in terms of psychological needs or social processes.

I have not abandoned my rationality or the search for truth expressed in ways that are intelligible to the sharpest human mind. God does not want us to cease using our minds. But he has added a new dimension to my thinking; it is that of a dynamic faith rooted in a personal experience of the living Christ and the constant ministry of the Holy Spirit. It is out of this experience that this book has flowed.

I am most grateful to the Reverend Gilbert Kirby for writing the Foreword to this book and for all his encouragement and support in my ministry, and to Mrs Jean Wolton who typed the text with speed and efficiency.

It is my earnest prayer that I have been faithful to God in what has been written.

Clifford Hill
January 1983

CHAPTER ONE

Adelboden

I would rank high in the ratings for the world's worst skier. As soon as I strap on a pair of skis my body displays an irresistible urge to lie down. Even at speed I perform better upon that part of my body designed for sitting than upon those parts designed for standing. I might gain a few marks for persistence or even a sympathetic round of applause for courage in the face of adversity. But nobody in his right mind would link me with the world's top skiers!

It seemed strange therefore that in the middle of January my wife and I should be heading for Switzerland, to the very place where the Men's Downhill event of the World Cup was to be held. We were going, not as tourists, but by special invitation. The invitation, however, was not to the ski bonanza but to be speakers at the European Convention of the National Directors of Campus Crusade. We went there thinking of the World Cup as a happy coincidence and came away convinced that it was part of a larger plan for our lives.

The conference was held at a Christian centre on the outskirts of the little town of Adelboden, nestling on the side of a mountain high up in the Swiss Alps. The snowcovered slopes, picturesque valley and majestic peaks visible from our bedroom window provided breathtaking views that spoke to us of the majesty and magnificence of our God. On the day of the World Cup I was speaking at the morning session and we were both due to speak at the evening meeting, but the afternoon was free. So we set out to walk the two miles from the conference centre through the town and along the mountain path to the slope where the competition was to be held.

On the way there I had a growing awareness of the

presence of God, and it wasn't just a spiritual response to the beauty and grandeur of the scenery. I have learned to distinguish the times when God draws particularly close to communicate a special message, and have learned at those times to be especially attentive and watchful. So it was with a heightened sense of perception and expectancy that we arrived at the foot of the slope and joined the huge crowds that had gathered to watch some of the world's most daring and skilful young men risking life and limb to hurl themselves down the mountainside, trying to reduce record-breaking times by mere fractions of a second. It was a thrilling sight and we entered fully into the spirit of the occasion, cheering the Swiss boys popular with the local crowd (there being no British competitors!).

My wife and I have always enjoyed most forms of sport, both as participants and as spectators, but this afternoon was different. I had a strangely compelling feeling that there was some other reason why we had come out there. It wasn't just to see the Men's Downhill skiing event. I was sure that God had something to say to me, and I eagerly watched each swaying movement of the competitors racing down and even scanned the crowds around me for anything of significance through which God could be communicating with me.

Eventually it was all over. The last competitor completed his run, the presentations were made, the TV camera crews closed the eyes of the world and began stowing their equipment into the waiting trucks. We, along with several thousand other people, began to walk back into the town. As we turned away from the scene of action I found myself saying, 'Lord, have I missed something? Did I not have my eyes open to what you wanted to show me? What did you want me to see, Lord? Forgive me if I've not been attentive.'

The path back into Adelboden is narrow and winding, clinging around the side of the mountain. It was fairly slow going, with a large crowd threading its way along the snow-packed, icy track, which in some places is only four or five feet wide. At one point, where the pathway turns a sharp bend around the mountain, there is a low wooden guardrail, on the other side of which a very steep snowcovered slope runs for about a hundred feet to the edge of a precipice before a sheer drop of some five hundred feet on to the rocks below.

We had hardly turned the corner when the air was rent with the piercing scream of a child just behind me. She had evidently missed her footing coming round the bend on the outside of the crowd, slipped under the guardrail and was now sliding fast down that steep slope towards the edge of the precipice. I swung round and, together with hundreds of others, stood frozen to the spot, helplessly watching the small figure of the three- or four-year-old girl sliding down the mountainside, on her stomach, feet first, with arms and legs outstretched, screaming with the full power of her lungs, her eyes looking imploringly upwards as she slipped. I doubt whether I shall ever forget the look of helpless terror in that child's eyes as her body gathered speed on its way down towards certain death.

Before I could even gather my wits to take in the full horror of the sight, another dramatic event was to leave an indelible picture in my mind. Within seconds, whilst the first screams from the child were echoing across the valley, a man hurled himself through the crowd, leapt the guardrail and ran down the slope with such incredible speed that he rapidly began to overtake the child, who was still slithering downwards screaming at the top of her voice.

It was little short of a miracle how he kept his balance on that acute slope, actually running down the mountainside. A few more strides and he passed the child, then managed to stop himself in a flurry of snow and moments later caught her as she reached him, only some ten feet short of the precipice. He gathered the little girl up into his arms, while she in turn flung her arms around his neck and clung tightly to him sobbing loudly, but now with a very different tone.

The man, whom I took to be the child's father, stood there for a few moments regaining his breath and steadying himself in preparation for the highly dangerous climb back up the snowcovered slope. Then, with the child in his arms, his heavy ski boots digging deeply into the snow, he began the

11

slow tortuous ascent to safety, travelling sideways to cope with the extra weight and testing each fresh foothold before taking a full step. Eventually he reached the barrier – where plenty of willing hands stretched out to help him on to the pathway and to lift the little girl over the rail and into the comfort of her mother's arms.

As I watched the father standing there so close to the sheer drop on to the rocks below, and as I watched him begin his slow ascent with the child in his arms, I very clearly heard God saying to me, 'This is what I brought you here to see. You saw how that child was sliding towards certain destruction. You saw how her eyes were looking up to her father, and you heard how she cried out for help. You saw how her father responded immediately, not hesitating to assess the danger to himself, but flung himself down the mountainside to rescue his child. That is how I love my children.'

'Lord, that is wonderful!' I replied. 'That is wonderful.' Immediately, I felt him speak again but this time they were words of rebuke. 'Why?' said the Lord. 'Why do you say, "That is wonderful"? Do you think that I would do less than a human father? Did I not create him? Did I not make that father capable of such love for his child? Am I less than man, whom I made? Am I not God? There is no other! I created the ends of the earth and I created man in my own image. Did not my Beloved Son tell you that the servant is not above his master?

'I made man capable of the saving love you have witnessed this afternoon. I put my love within him. My love for all my children is as great as that father's love for his child and a million times more! And a million times more than that! Did not my Beloved Son go to the limits of the Cross for you? Why do you doubt my love?'

I felt him reminding me:

> Mine is an unchanging love
> Higher than the heights above
> Deeper than the depths beneath.

Then came the very clear words, 'Tell my people I love them.'

I walked down the path and into the town completely oblivious of the crowds around me, lost in wonder, love and praise. In that little human drama of saving love I had witnessed a tiny glimpse of God's great saving purposes for his children and had heard him speak to me. The fresh mountain air, the winding path, the breathtaking view across the valley, all seemed to take on a new significance, transformed by an awareness of the presence of the living God. I felt I understood something of Moses's experience on another mountain, when he took off his shoes feeling that the very ground on which he stood was holy with the presence of Almighty God.

As I walked through the town, again and again I heard him saying to me, 'Tell my people I love them. Tell my people I love them.' The experience of that afternoon on the mountainside transformed the evening message. It brought something of the power of the presence of the living God into the gathering of his children that added a fresh dynamic to the word.

It is because the awareness of the presence of the risen Christ is so often lacking when we meet in his name that we have transformed what should be a celebration of his presence and power into the dull routine of religious observance. When we do realize his presence and we lift up the name of Jesus and glorify him, there is a power let loose that goes beyond anything we could ever imagine. His presence brings such unutterable beauty, peace and joy that we are left speechless and can only fall down and worship him. The realization of the presence of the living God brings a release of love into a gathering of his people that causes miracles to occur. These are the signs and wonders of his presence that Jesus tells us to expect and which accompany the preaching of the Gospel.

A few weeks after the Adelboden incident I was leading worship in a London church where the presence of the Lord Jesus was so powerful that he entered the experience of everyone present, believers and unbelievers alike. Following the preaching of the word, which had not been particularly eloquent, there was a time of open worship, and it was during this time that the presence of the living God was so powerfully felt. At the normal end of the service I tried to close the worship. I pronounced the benediction, walked out of the church and stood in the porch by the main doors to greet people on their way home. But nobody moved. The whole congregation went on spontaneously worshipping the Lord. Not a single person got up and left the church. After several minutes standing there on my own I said to myself, 'Why should I be out here on my own when they're all in there getting blessed?' So I went back into the church and joined in. Six people committed their lives to Christ that night and several people were healed, including a man with a broken arm.

There were no hysterical scenes. There was no great emotion. No one danced in the aisle or walked across the ceiling. But the presence of the living Lord Jesus was such a reality that everyone was blessed. There were little groups of praying people all around the church, and every now and again there broke out a scripture chorus or song of praise that gripped the whole congregation. Occasionally someone would say that there had been a healing or a conversion and the whole company rejoiced. One example was of the man who had come in with a broken arm; he came to the front to testify to the power and love of God. He raised his arms in praise and said, 'Look, I can even scratch the back of my head!' And we all rejoiced and gave glory to God.

It was eleven thirty at night before the church was finally cleared and the last person went home. But why should this be so unusual? After all, who wants to go and watch TV when Jesus is present among his people? Who can wish for anything more wonderful or more exhilarating than when the presence of the living God is experienced among his people and there is an outpouring of his love into their lives? The world has nothing to offer so amazing or so richly satisfying.

In my own ministry the experience I've just described in

that London church has occurred so many times that it's become almost commonplace. But why should we regard such happenings as unusual? Surely the whole purpose of worship is to lift up the name of Jesus and to glorify him. When we do this and his presence and power are released among us there is an outpouring of his love that heals our broken relationships, that brings wholeness to our spirits, healing to our bodies and the restoration of our peace with God our Father and Creator. We regard healings as abnormal instead of being the everyday occurrences to be expected when Jesus is present with his people. The man with the broken arm did not come to the front and become the object of a public spectacle, with the laying-on of hands or anointing with oil or the offering up of special prayers. He was in the back row when he was healed, and he only came forward in order to make an open testimony and to give all the glory to God. When Jesus is present everyone gets blessed, and all those who ask in faith receive according to their need. This is the evidence of his love. It is the love of the father who delights to please his children, to give good gifts to those who trust him and who respond to his fatherly love.

Jesus said, 'What human father whose son asks him for a loaf of bread would give him a stone? Or if he asks for fish would give him a scorpion? If you know how to give good gifts to your children how much more shall your heavenly father give to you.' Jesus was continually emphasizing God's fatherly love and care for all his people; it was this message of God's unchanging love that Jesus entrusted to his followers after his own greatest act of self-giving love on the Cross. Yet in a world that is hungry for love today we grossly neglect the central theme of the Gospel: God's redeeming, all-embracing, utterly limitless love. Why is it that in a world of fear – when only love casts out fear – and in a world of violence – that can only be overcome by love – we have so grossly neglected the central dynamic of the Gospel?

It is in an attempt to recover the centrality of the love of God as the basic dynamic of the Gospel that I have in these chapters undertaken this exploration of the fatherly love of God. The purpose also is to witness to the belief that God is urgently communicating his love to his people in days of mounting world crisis.

CHAPTER TWO

The Love of God

The experience of that afternoon on the mountainside at Adelboden was unforgettable but it also has great personal significance for me. The sight of that father running down the snowcovered slope towards the edge of the precipice is indelibly etched into my memory. It has given me a new understanding of the love of God in action through the Cross. I have asked myself a hundred times, 'If that had been my child slipping down the mountainside towards certain death, woud I have run after her to try to save her?' I know it's really an impossible question to ask since none of us knows how we would react under the extreme pressures of such an emergency. I would like to think that I would have gone to rescue my own child. I can't be sure; but I believe I would have tried.

The one thing I do know for sure is that I did not attempt to rescue the little girl who actually did slip under the guardrail. That is the awful truth that really stuns me. I actually stood there, along with a large crowd of other men, and simply watched the child sliding towards her death. I did nothing about it. Neither did all the other men around me. Only one man moved to risk his life in a rescue bid.

Why did not I leap the guardrail and rush to her aid in response to those penetrating screams and pleading eyes? The answer is simple although I don't like it: I didn't go because I did not love enough. It is love that motivates you to risk your life in a death-defying endeavour to save a life. It is love that overcomes my natural fear and my instinctive wish for self-preservation. It is love that drives me to do something my reason tells me is crazy, is irrational, is against my self-interest. It is love that makes a man willing to lay down his life for another.

The shattering truth is that while I might possibly risk my life to save my own child, I did nothing to save someone else's child. The more I think about this fact the more unlovely I find myself and the more lovely I find the Lord Jesus, who was not only willing to die but actually did die for me. I see myself as that helpless child sliding towards destruction and the Lord Jesus rushing to snatch me to safety.

> You see, at just the right time, when we were still powerless, Christ died for the ungodly. Very rarely will anyone die for a righteous man, though for a good man someone might possibly dare to die. But God demonstrates his own love for us in this: while we were still sinners Christ died for us. (Romans 5:6–8)

It is as though saving me on the mountainside Christ went over the precipice himself as that was the only way he could ensure my certain rescue.

What incredible love for one so unlovely as me! 'Amazing love, how can it be that thou my God shouldst die for me!' That is the strength and power and limitless length of the Father's love for us his children. It is this love that inspired the preaching of John Wesley and the hymns of Charles Wesley, and that spread the fire of revival throughout Britain. It is this love that so many Christians have lost sight of today. It is this love that God is urgently communicating to us afresh in these days of mounting world crisis.

Jesus constantly taught his disciples to think of God as Father: to pray to him as Father; and to understand his nature in terms of the highest and best attributes of a human father. 'Which of you, if his son asks for bread, will give him a stone? Or if he asks for a fish, will give him a snake? If you, then, though you are evil, know how to give good gifts to your children, how much more will your father in heaven give good gifts to those who ask him!' (Matthew 7:9–11).

I was preaching in a church in California soon after the Adelboden incident. I said that the action of that father, rushing to save his child and snatch her from the jaws of death regardless of the danger to his own life, spoke to me vividly of God's action through the Cross in dying for us through Jesus. Afterwards several people came up and told me that they had never thought of God dying for us through Jesus but only of God punishing Jesus for our sins.

These people, and many others like them, are victims of the distortions of evangelical theology which has so stressed 'penal substitution' that it has produced a division within the Godhead, a kind of dualism. The witness of the New Testament does not show God to be an angry judge standing over Jesus, demanding a perfect sacrifice on behalf of the guilty to satisfy his outraged righteousness. The witness of scripture is that 'God was in Christ reconciling the world to himself, not counting their trespasses against them' (2 Corinthians 5:19). The moment we cease to recognize the saving action of God himself through the death of Jesus on the Cross, we cease to present a true biblical witness. We distort the Gospel and misrepresent the true nature of God to the world.

Multitudes of men and women have been lost through inadequate theological teaching or have suffered unnecessary agonies of mind and spirit through unbalanced and distorted teaching. Whilst preparing the notes for this book, I received a letter from a man whom I had never met, appealing for help – he is a victim of acute depression. He had been converted in a Brethren assembly and had learned first to fear God and then to hate him. He was now plunging headlong towards a nervous breakdown, tormented by terrible guilt because he felt he hated God. 'But', he asked, 'how can I love a loveless monster? I see God as an awful, monstrous, disinterested God who will do nothing for anyone and finally dooms the majority of humanity to everlasting burning. The "God is love" bit is a con to get a few stupid sheep round himself. If he *is* love no one would know it; he's not evident in human life in any way other than disaster, death and judgement.'

His letter showed an extensive but highly selective knowledge of scripture which he quoted freely, always showing God as cruel, vengeful, judgemental and uncaring; a God even delighting in the punishment of the weak. He wrote: 'It appears from Revelation that the weak and fearful (cowardly) are cast into the lake of fire. At the same time God commands Christians to comfort and succour the weak. How can he expect this when instead of taking a weak, fearful person into his (so-called) loving arms, he burns him for ever? What possible advantage can it have to God or the person involved? I cannot see how this could help me to love this God who now appears to me to be a monster worse than Satan himself. The wickedness of burning the weak, faithless, cowards, for eternity is far worse than the extermination of six million Jews by the Nazis. It makes that look like a Sunday school picnic.' He ends with the plea, again: 'God commands us to love him, but how can I love a loveless monster?'

I do not wish to imply that all Brethren assemblies are guilty of presenting a distorted image of God, but clearly the man who wrote to me had not received sound biblical teaching. He was a living proof of the old maxim that truth over-emphasized becomes error. In biblical terms, partial truth, over-emphasized in isolation from the whole witness of scripture, becomes error. All too often the judgement and the love of God are taught in isolation, as separate entities within the divine nature, instead of in creative fusion as inseparable characteristics within the nature of God. Thus the way is left open for heavy stress, or even exclusive concentration, upon either justice or love according to the whim, or even some deep-seated emotional foible, of the teacher.

One of the saddest features of the modern Christian scene is the way our divisions have given rise to so many different and partial theologies which distort the nature of God. Thus we have an 'evangelical theology' which emphasizes the sinfulness of man and God's action in redemption and salvation. In theological terms the evangelical emphasis tends to be upon the righteousness and judgement of God. In contrast 'liberal theology' takes a more optimistic view of man and concentrates upon his capacity for goodness when harnessed to the good purposes of God. Liberal theology tends therefore to emphasize the goodness, forgivingness and loving-kindness of God. Both views contain some biblical truth, but each expresses only a partial reflection of the whole nature of God. There are today so many different theologies that it is small wonder many people get confused and lost along the way. In addition to evangelical and liberal theology there is liberation theology, social action theology, charismatic theology, eschatological theology, restoration theology, submission theology, holiness theology, dispensational theology and black theology!

What is most urgently needed today is a full biblical theology, that is, a theology which will adequately reflect the whole biblical tradition in regard to the nature of God. I have no doubt that one of the reasons why the heretical cults are able to lead so many people astray today is because people are already confused by the immense number of different denominations, sects and independent groups, each emphasizing some different aspect of biblical truth. We urgently need a fresh attempt to set aside the old prejudices and preconceived doctrinal positions, with their blinkered partiality and inflexibility. We need to discover afresh the nature of God from the whole biblical tradition. I believe that the first thing we should discover from such a biblical quest is that recent theological study has grossly neglected an understanding of the love of God.

I believe that God himself is crying out to us today to rediscover his love, to try to understand the height and breadth, the length and depth of the love of God our father. Of course there will be those who will immediately object that you cannot have the love of God without the justice and judgement. This is perfectly true, but the statement in itself reveals an inadequate understanding of the nature of God's love. His love *contains* justice and righteousness, it *contains* holiness and the bringing of sinners to repentance. These are all *elements* within the divine love. But they are each partial elements and not the whole. They are aspects of love and activities of it, rather than fundamental attributes of the divine nature in isolation from each other. It is only love that the Bible reveals as being the fundamental nature of God. It is love that is the all-embracing, indivisible essential attribute of the Godhead.

God is love. The Bible bears witness to this from beginning to end. When God 'proclaimed his name' or revealed the fundamental qualities of his nature to Moses, he revealed himself as 'the compassionate and gracious God, slow to anger, abounding in love and faithfulness, maintaining love to thousands, and forgiving wickedness, rebellion and sin' (Exodus 34:6 and 7).

Throughout their history God continually reminded the Israelites of his great love for them. 'The Lord did not set his affection on you and choose you because you were more numerous than other peoples, for you were the fewest of all peoples. But it was because the Lord loved you and kept the oath he swore to your forefathers that he brought you out with a mighty hand and redeemed you from the land of slavery . . . he is the faithful God keeping his covenant of love to a thousand generations of those who love him and keep his commands' (Deuteronomy 7:7–9).

The same witness comes clearly through the ministry of the prophets. Hosea, whose wife was faithless, learned from his own suffering and bitter experience in marriage how much God loves his faithless and sinful children. If Hosea could love an adulterous woman who continually forsook him for other lovers, how much more did God love and continually forgive and redeem his own wayward children. God is at least as good as the best human husband. To say God is less is a blasphemy against his nature and a denial of his whole activity in creation. Either we believe God has created man in his own image and therefore made him capable of love, compassion, forgiveness and mercy, or we deny the very fabric of creation and the biblical witness of God's activity and place in his own universe. Hosea's own witness is 'The Lord said to me, "Go show your love to your wife again, though she is loved by another and is an adultress. Love her as the Lord loves the Israelites"' (Hosea 3:1).

Isaiah rebukes those who were suffering during the exile and who were saying that the Lord had forsaken and forgotten them. He protests, 'Can a mother forget the baby at her breast and have no compassion on the child she has borne? Though she may forget, I will not forget you! See, I have engraved you on the palms of my hands; your walls are ever before me' (Isaiah 49:15 and 16). He uses the poignant illustration of a mother suckling her infant child, for whom it is virtually impossible to forget her baby, since her breasts refill every few hours to remind her of him. Yet God's love and unforgetfulness is even greater and more certain than the mother's for her baby. Because she is human, it is just possible that she may be forgetful under the pressure of other demands. But God is not like that. He is not subject to human pressures. Nothing can distract him or turn him aside from his loving care for his people. If it seems impossible for the mother to forget her infant child, it is a million times more impossible for God to forget his children.

'See,' he says, 'I have engraved you on the palms of my hands.' It was the practice of the people, when they had a special prayer request, to write on their hands the name of the person for whom they were interceding. Then, when they held up their hands in prayer they were, symbolically, lifting up that person before the Lord. God says to his people that he had not merely written their names upon the palms of his hands but has actually engraved them there. Nothing can remove them. They are permanently before him even in their suffering and brokenness. This thought is clearly conveyed in the words 'your walls are ever before me', when God was referring to the walls of Jerusalem which, of course, were non-existent – or at least were in crumbling ruins since their destruction by Nebuchadnezzar. The charred stones and blackened ruins, symbols of the suffering of the Lord's people, were continually before him.

Four chapters later Isaiah reveals the extent to which God enters into and shares in our human sorrow and suffering. 'Surely he took up our infirmities and carried our sorrows, yet we considered him stricken by God, smitten by him and

23

afflicted. But he was pierced for our transgressions, he was crushed for our iniquities' (Isaiah 53:4 and 5). It is not until we reach the New Testament that this revelation given to Isaiah becomes understandable. When we interpret it in the light of Jesus's life, death and resurrection we catch a glimpse of God's great purposes in redeeming mankind through the Cross. In the Cross we see something of the cost to God of his great love for us as he took our sins upon himself.

The primary witness of the New Testament is to the love of God. It was for this purpose that Jesus came to the world – to reveal the fatherly nature of God, to make him known: 'No one has ever seen God, but God the only Son, who is at the Father's side, has made him known.' In his prayer to the Father shortly before the crucifixion Jesus spoke of the way he had revealed the Father to those who had responded to his ministry: 'I have made you known to them, and will continue to make you known in order that the love you have for me may be in them and that I myself may be in them' (John 17:26).

Jesus used numerous illustrations to demonstrate God's fatherly love and care. He taught his disciples to pray to God as 'Our Father', and he demonstrated the nature of that fatherhood through parables such as the three in Luke 15, 'the lost sheep', 'the lost coin' and 'the lost son'. Each of these illustrates the joy of the father at the return of his wayward children. That joy is epitomized in the action of the father in running to meet the lost son the moment he turned towards home, and in his total restoration to his position within the family despite the son's protests 'I am no longer worthy to be called your son', Jesus emphasized the unlimited compassion and abounding love of the father.

The New Testament shows God's love as not being confined to the followers of Jesus, although clearly there is a special relationship between them and God since they have responded to his love. But that love is available for anyone and everyone. 'For God so loved the world he gave his one and only Son, that whoever believes in him shall not perish but have eternal life' (John 3:16). Jesus makes it abundantly clear that there are no limitations on God's love. It is all-inclusive and he longs to include within his fatherly embrace every one of his children throughout the world, for he has created them in his own image, made them all capable of fellowship with him. Jesus underlines both the universality of God's love and his deep desire for every man, woman and child to come to know him and thereby to enter into a right relationship with him. 'For God did not send his Son into the world to condemn the world, but to save the world through him' (John 3:17).

In order to emphasize what this right relationship with the Father through the Son would mean, Jesus gave a solemn promise: 'If anyone loves me, he will obey my teaching. My Father will love him, and we will come to him and make our home with him' (John 14:23). That promise followed the promise to send the Holy Spirit to all those who respond to his love. 'If you love me, you will obey what I command. And I will ask the Father, and he will give you another Counsellor to be with you for ever – the spirit of truth' (John 14:15).

Those two promises, occurring in the same discourse, are a solemn undertaking that both the Father and the Son, through the power of the Holy Spirit, will come and dwell within the believer who turns to the Father as a faith response to the Son. It is love for which Jesus is looking, but love as a response to his own love for us. His promise is that he and the Father will make their permanent home with the believer – not just an overnight temporary stopover but a permanent abode, their unchanging, abiding presence.

For Paul the most amazing fact about God's love is that he loves us when we are so unlovely and so unworthy of that love. We are rebellious and sinful men and women, but nevertheless he loves us because we are his children. He says, 'Very rarely will anyone die for a righteous man, though for a good man someone might possibly dare to die. But God demonstrates his own love for us in this: while we were still sinners, God died for us' (Romans 5:7 and 8). Paul could never find words adequately to express the sheer wonder of the love of God, which simply passes human understanding.

His prayer for the Ephesians is, 'And I pray that you, being rooted and established in love, may have power, together with all the saints, to grasp how wide and long and high and deep is the love of Christ, and to know this love that surpasses knowledge – that you may be filled to the measure of all the fullness of God' (Ephesians 3:17–19). Although his mind could never fully grasp the extent of God's love or understand his loving compassion, he yet knew that love as a fact. Christ had reached out and touched him. The transformation in his life was total and complete. Jesus now had all of him and he knew from experience that nothing could separate him from the love of Christ. 'For I am convinced that neither death nor life, neither angels nor demons, neither the present nor the future, nor any powers, neither height nor depth, nor anything else in all creation, will be able to separate us from the love of God that is in Christ Jesus our Lord' (Romans 8:38 and 39).

It is the witness of scripture that we need to show love in all our relationships, both with God himself and with our fellow men and women. There are no limits to this love that we are expected to show, just as there are no limits to the love that God has for us. It is Jesus's commandment that we should even love our enemies. It is through such love that we become sons of God. 'But love your enemies, do good to them, and lend to them without expecting to get anything back. Then your reward will be great, and you will be sons of the most high, because he is kind to the ungrateful and wicked. Be merciful, just as your Father is merciful' (Luke 6:35 and 36).

It is notable that Jesus justifies his command to love those who do not love us, and even to love those who actually wish us harm, by saying that this is how God himself loves us. He loves the ungrateful and the wicked, and is merciful to them. The whole of the New Testament witness in regard to the love of God emphasizes that it is God who first loves us and that his love is free and totally undeserved. Our love for him is therefore a faith response to his own wondrous love for us. It is the very nature of God to love us because he in essence is love. When we love him, or when we show love to others, we are in fact reflecting his love. We are giving back to him the love he has already given to us or we are radiating his love to others around us.

John expresses this beautifully when he writes, 'Dear friends, let us love one another, for love comes from God. Everyone who loves has been born of God and knows God. Whoever does not know love does not know God, because God is love. This is how God showed his love among us; he sent his one and only Son into the world that we might live through him. This is love, not that we loved God, but that he loved us and sent his Son as an atoning sacrifice for our sins. Dear friends, since God so loved us, we also ought to love one another' (1 John 4:7–11). John adds, 'God is love. Whoever lives in love lives in God and God in him . . . We love because he first loved us' (1 John 4:16 and 19).

CHAPTER THREE

The Witness of the Spirit

God is speaking to us of his love today with a new urgency. This is not just because so much of our theological emphases have been shallow and inadequate in recent times, but because he is longing to draw us closer to himself in love and trust so that he can speak to us and use us in this present period of world history.

In order to communicate clearly with us, as the world moves steadily into deepening days of crisis and the clouds above us become ever darker, God is urgently calling upon us to lift up our eyes and look to him. With the kind of saturation news coverage that we have in the Western world we can say that most people are aware of events in the world around us, although very few realize their full significance. Even among those most aware of what is happening there is a great reluctance to admit the acute danger facing mankind. Even among Christians there is a reluctance to turn to God in child-like dependence and in recognition that only he can save the world from a disaster beyond the capacity of the human mind to imagine or describe, to give to the world the witness that is needed.

It is for this reason that God is raising up prophets today to speak directly to his people. Of course the world doesn't recognize them. That's hardly surprising because the world doesn't want to acknowledge God, so why should worldly men heed his word? But what is much more sad, and could have tragic consequences for our world, is that some Christians find it hard to believe that God speaks through prophets today.

There is a widely held belief that the ministry of the prophet ceased at the end of the New Testament period of the Church. The most frequently quoted passage of scripture offered in support of this view is Paul's statement in 1 Corinthians 13 that the day will come when prophecies will cease and tongues will be stilled and knowledge will pass away. He says

> for we know in part and we prophesy in part, but when perfection comes, the imperfect disappears.
>
> (1 Corinthians 13:9 and 10)

The coming of that which is perfect has been interpreted (and in my view misinterpreted) as meaning the completion of the writing of scripture. Those who hold this view say that once the Bible was given to us there was no further need for prophets. They overlook two vital facts. The first is that 1 Corinthians 13 is about love, not about the writing of the Bible. Paul is looking forward to the day when the love of God will be established among men through his kingly rule and glorification upon earth, which can only refer to the Second Coming of our Lord and the establishment of his messianic reign.

> Now we see but a poor reflection: then we shall see face to face. Now I know in part; then I shall know fully, even as I am fully known. (v. 12)

It also overlooks the fact that there is plenty of evidence for the exercise of the ministry of prophets within the Church long after the last of the books of our Bible had been written.

Jesus clearly expected the ministry of the prophets to continue – he said: 'Whoever receives a prophet will receive a prophet's reward' – as did other major New Testament writers such as Paul and John. They give clear instructions on how to handle prophecy. Paul says that when a prophet speaks 'the others should weigh carefully what is said' (1 Corinthians 14:29). John gives a clear warning against the uncritical acceptance of everything that purports to be prophecy.

Do not believe every spirit, but test the spirits to see
whether they are from God, because many false prophets
have gone out into the world. (1 John 4:1)

John goes on in the same passage to give instructions on how
to recognize false prophecy from the truth. Paul, while
admonishing Christians in the churches he founded to test
prophecy, nevertheless warned them against keeping their
minds closed to the Holy Spirit speaking through prophets.

Do not put out the Spirit's fire; do not treat prophecies
with contempt. Test everything. Hold on to the good.
Avoid every kind of evil. (1 Thessalonians 5:19-22)

In times of crisis God frequently gives a new movement of
the Holy Spirit and speaks to his people directly through the
prophetic word. Such words, if they are of God, will not
contradict scripture in any way, neither will they add to
scripture. No one can do this, for scripture is the inspired
word of God. It is complete and cannot be either added to
or subtracted from. It contains all that is necessary for our
salvation. Yet while holding this view of the uniqueness of
scripture we are not prevented from believing that other
words may be inspired by God, although we do not elevate
them to a par with scripture. It is surely indisputable that in
the gospels we have recorded for us only a tiny fraction of the
words that Jesus spoke during his earthly life and ministry.
Yet surely no one would dare to say that the many other
words that Jesus spoke either to the crowds or to his own
disciples were not inspired by the Holy Spirit.

I believe that same Holy Spirit is with us today. The
evidence of his presence and power is all around us. Those
who have eyes to see will see, but those who are blinded to
the work of the Holy Spirit will remain in their ignorance and
will not enter into the fullness of blessing that God is giving
to his people today. They will also miss the mighty works
that God is doing among his people and will fail to be a part
of the great army of witnesses that he is raising in the world.

The ministry of the prophet is not one to be taken lightly, neither is it to be sought after. Indeed it is quite the reverse. It is one of the greatest burdens that any man can have laid upon him. It is not something a man strives after but rather something he implores the Lord to take away, to release him from its burden. If anyone doubts the truth of this let him read the experience of Jeremiah recorded for us in chapter twenty of that prophet's writing. Jeremiah was beaten and put into the stocks for bringing an unpopular prophecy against the city of Jerusalem. The first six verses show both the faithfulness and the courage of the prophet. Verses 7 and 8 are a strong contrast and show the depths of despair and self-doubt into which the prophet could be plunged. Verse 9 shows the struggle within him and the impossibility of running away from the ministry that was laid upon him.

If I say, 'I will not mention him, or speak any more in his name', there is in my heart as it were a burning fire shut up in my bones, and I am weary with holding it in, and I cannot.

Verses 10 to 13 show the prophet under attack when it looks as though the enemy will overwhelm him; but faith finally triumphs. Then in verses 14 to 18 he is plunged into the depths of self-loathing and reels under the impact of the burden of the prophetic ministry:

Cursed be the day on which I was born! The day when my mother bore me, let it not be blest! Cursed be the man who brought the news to my father, 'a son is born to you', making him very glad. Let that man be like the cities which the Lord overthrew without pity; let him hear a cry in the morning and an alarm at noon, because he did not kill me in the womb; so my mother would have been my grave, and her womb forever great. Why did I come forth from the womb to see toil and sorrow and to spend my days in shame?

Jeremiah reveals the agony of the prophet, who longs to be rid of the burden he is carrying but is compelled by an inner force that he can neither control nor explain to speak the word of God that has been laid upon him. He longs for release yet cannot be other than faithful. His greatest human desire is to be like other men and to live a normal life. But there is a greater desire within him that is irresistible: the desire to please the Lord, to be obedient to him and to be faithful in the task he has been given. He is a messenger of God, and to keep silent would not only be a dereliction of duty but would be to deny the reality of the living God who had spoken to him and given him the message. For the prophet that is the most intense reality in his life. It becomes an irresistible compulsion that cannot be disobeyed. Even though men scoff and he becomes the object of ridicule he cannot cease to bear witness to the word of God that has been given to him.

The ministry of the prophet today is in some ways even more difficult than that of the great prophets of the Old Testament. They were prophesying to a nation that was in a covenant relationship with God. That nation had an identity, a common heritage and geographical limits. The prophet of today has to speak to a people who have no social identity. They are a people who stand in a covenant relationship with God as did the people of the old Israel, but they are not a nation in the human sense. They are a nation within the nations, drawn from among all the nations. Their unity is a spiritual unity and their identity is that of a common belongingness to Christ as Saviour through their acceptance of Jesus as Lord. Those who once were not a people are now God's people (1 Peter 2:10). They have been bound together in a new unity through the work of the Holy Spirit. Although they speak many different languages and represent many diverse cultures they are a single people, 'a chosen race, a royal priesthood, a holy nation, God's own people' (1 Peter 2:9).

Despite the advances in technology and the ease of modern communications, the task of speaking to such a diverse company as God's people of the new covenant in the twentieth century is daunting. But the major problem is not simply a difficulty of communication. It is the problem of credibility within such diversity. Yet, essentially, this is not part of the prophet's burden. He has to learn to leave that with God. His task is simply to be faithful to God, to speak only that which he has been given and to bear witness to the truth as it has been revealed to him. When he carries out this task without fear of the consequences and without regard to personal status or heeding the wounds that come from the world and from God's people he then knows the prophet's reward – that of a close walk with God.

There is a single-mindedness about the ministry of the prophet. It is not the usual directness of the dedicated person who is committed to carrying out a specific task. It is the single-mindedness of the man of God whose life is consumed by the words he has been given. When the hand of the Lord is upon him he sees no objects and fears no enemy and has but one desire – to be obedient to the Lord and to speak aloud what he has heard within.

He is subject to the black despair of self-doubt when he is under the intense assault of the enemy, but the reality of the presence of God and the knowledge of his commission never leave him. Faith triumphs over personal weakness and, in the precious moments of anointing, the Spirit carries him and compels him in a way that surpasses human understanding. He learns not to strive for the agreement of men or for acceptability but only to walk in obedience and to leave the witness of the Spirit to speak to those who are numbered among the people of God.

The ministry of the prophet is not one into which a man is appointed by a committee or by a body of men or even by the whole Church. Neither is it a status which a man claims for himself. It is an anointing of God that becomes apparent in a man's ministry, in the words that he speaks, and in his life. I was exercising a 'prophetic ministry' and being spoken of as a prophet long before I acknowledged the ministry myself. Many times I have run away from it. I have tried to keep quiet and have refused to speak even when I knew the Lord was giving me a word. But the word of the Lord is irresistible. When his hand is upon you, though you run away, you will be restrained. The word within you becomes a compelling force that cannot be contained. I think the most difficult lesson for me to learn has been that of absolute obedience. It has not been easy because I am by nature a very self-willed and headstrong character. Yet if spiritual obedience is the mark of the disciple it is the absolute pre-requisite of the ministry of the prophet. He not only has to learn to listen and be attentive to each detail of what the Lord is saying, but he also has to learn to abide in his timing.

God spoke to me very clearly about timing some years ago. He gave me a picture of a beach where there were huge waves rolling in from the ocean. There were a lot of people there on the beach, many of them with surf boards. I watched them plunging out into the water, carrying their surf boards with them. Some of them were going out a very long way to where the great waves were rising, sending up huge plumes of white foam spray. I watched the surf riders jumping and trying to catch the crest of the wave. Many of them were being knocked over by the powerful impact of a great wave upon their body, while others just seemed to disappear in the fine white spray which passed over their heads. I felt the Lord pointing out to me that these unsuccessful riders were jumping too soon and being swamped by the force of the waves breaking over them. Others were jumping too late, when the main thrust of the wave had already passed them, and there was no power to carry them.

As I watched I saw one surf rider jump at exactly the right moment and with his board he mounted right up to the very crest of the wave. He was carried by its immense power, triumphant in the midst of its dazzling white spray, all the way back to the land. I heard the Lord saying to me, 'Did you see how that man jumped at exactly the right moment so that he was carried by the full force of the wave? That is how I will carry you if you will wait for my timing. Do not go too soon, neither lag behind when I give the word, but wait upon me for my perfect timing, then when you speak you will be heard, for the word will not be yours but mine.'

Since then I have been storing up many things that the Lord has shown me and awaiting his perfect timing. Early in 1979 I received a vision of which I have never spoken in public until now. For a long time I believed that I never would speak of it. Even now I do so with reluctance and only under a strong sense of compulsion. My reluctance stems in part from a natural reticence to reveal in public a part of my private walk with the Lord that for me has very great significance. It is like allowing the public into the inner sanctuary of my private prayer life – my own personal holy of holies. It feels as though I am revealing for general gaze one of the most holy and precious experiences of my life.

The only thing that overcomes my reluctance is the fear of disobedience. I believe I know a little of the experience of the old Quakers who got their nickname as 'God Quakers' through their fearlessness under persecution and their fear of the Lord. They were unafraid of anything the world did to them but they quaked in the presence of Almighty God.

Some time ago I discovered a verse in Psalm 32 that has come to mean a great deal to me. Through it God gives a promise:

> I will instruct you and teach you in the way you should go;
> I will counsel you and watch over you.   (v. 8)

I have claimed that promise for the ministry that God has given me and through it have many times proved the faithfulness of the Lord.

I have already confessed to the difficulties I experienced in learning obedience. Just before I began writing this book I had a further such lesson to learn. I received a pressing invitation to go and lead a two-day retreat for the staff of the Prison Christian Fellowship at a centre in southern England. The engagement had been 'pencilled' in my diary for several months but for some reason it had not been confirmed and I tried very hard to get out of it. I needed the time. I was immersed in a very busy period of ministry. I argued with God and almost pleaded with those who'd invited me to release me. But in the end I went and the Lord was present in a very wonderful way. Quite apart from the fact that he used me to minister into the lives of those present, he spoke to me very clearly. I came away greatly blessed and from that moment began to step out in faith in a new phase of public ministry assured of his presence and his power in my life.

It was at this retreat that the Lord gave me the sign that resulted in the writing of this book. He also gave me a promise through which he confirmed that the time had come to begin to speak of the things he had been showing me for several years and that now have to be conveyed to the Body of Christ in this generation. When I look back I tremble to think that I almost missed the experience that provided the vital link in the chain of my ministry. I nearly missed it through a failure to discern the significance of one engagement in an overfull diary. I was so committed to the things I thought were important that I was not listening attentively. Sometimes we can become so busy that we haven't time to stop and listen to the things that God is saying to us. When we do this we place ourselves in great danger of missing his perfect timing.

I will always be grateful to one of the trustees of the Prison Christian Fellowship, whom I love and respect, but against whom I felt some resentment at the time, for his persistence in telling me that he had a strong witness in his spirit that I should go to the retreat. It was his 'strong witness' that made me take the whole matter before the Lord and pray it through. In the end I had to admit that I hadn't a single valid reason for not going. I went, although with a spirit of heaviness, and with no real expectation of the wonderful things that God was to do during those two days.

How easy it is to shut ourselves out from the place of his blessing! How easy it is to be so busy doing those things that we believe are his will that we haven't time to stop and listen to the new direction he is giving us! Every time I think I have learned the lesson of spiritual obedience and attentiveness to the promptings of the Spirit I find I have to start all over again. Gently, but firmly, he shows me that even in the central places of my discipleship I am not being fully obedient and my attentiveness leaves much to be desired.

I believe this disobedience and inattentiveness is characteristic of the whole Church today. We tend to get a little bit of the truth that has been neglected by previous generations and we pursue it relentlessly until we get it out of balance with the rest of scripture and our theology becomes distorted. We grasp hold of one tiny bit of God's great purposes for mankind, and for the Church, and for our own lives; then we devote all our energies unstintingly in that direction to the exclusion of all else; we fail to heed the warnings of the Spirit that we are moving outside his perfect will and exposing ourselves to the onslaught of the enemy. If we persist, we walk in our own strength and not his. Finally he has to break us of our self-will and our blindness before he can bring us back into the place of his blessing.

That really is the story of my own life, except that there have been, not just one, but numerous breaking points and the filling and refilling of the Holy Spirit. Maybe I am exceptionally stubborn, but I have found it all too easy to be carried away by my own enthusiasm along channels that take me out of the central stream of his perfect will. There have been two major breaking experiences in my life and I have discovered that being filled with the Holy Spirit is not a once in a lifetime event as I at first thought. I suppose it is wrong to be surprised at this. After all, what car owner is still running on the original tankful of fuel? The more journeys you undertake in your car the more you need to refill the tank. I believe we need to ask the Lord every day to be refilled with the Holy Spirit. Maybe the old hymn is right:

> I need thee every hour, most gracious Lord;
> No tender voice like thine can peace afford.
> I need thee every hour, in joy or pain;
> Come quickly and abide, or life is vain.

I was twelve years of age when I had my first experience of the presence of the living God. It was an awesome experience that brought about both my conversion and my initial commissioning. It was not until later years that I realized how remarkable the experience had been, since I had never seen anyone converted and no one had ever spoken to me about conversion. The church I attended with my parents was neither pentecostal nor evangelical. It was a conventional middle-of-the-road Protestant church with a deadly dull diet of worship, where no one ever got converted. There was never 'an appeal' for personal commitment and no tradition of biblical preaching or teaching. Yet I myself was steeped in scripture from my mother's faithful teaching. She had taught me many of the great stories of the Bible before I was old enough to read them for myself, and it was undoubtedly her gentle ministry that prepared me for the experience soon after my twelfth birthday.

It was a Saturday afternoon. I had gone to our local church with my parents to help prepare for the harvest thanksgiving services on the following day. After a while I made my way alone up into the back gallery. How long I was there I have no idea but it was during this time that I had an intense experience of the presence of God. I heard him speaking to me, saying that he was calling me to preach his word and was appointing me to fulfil a special ministry.

Later that day I told my mother what had happened to me and my response. She was a saintly woman with a deep prayer life, living in the daily presence of God. She showed no surprise at the things I told her and she then told me for the first time of certain things in her own spiritual life, of her expectations for me from before my birth and of how she had given me to the Lord at the time of my birth. She then instructed me not to tell anyone of what had happened and that in his own good time, God would make clear the meaning of the experience I had received. I have never, in fact, spoken of these things in public until this day, having always felt the restraining hand of the Lord upon me.

I quickly returned to the schoolboy world of mathematics

and marbles, but the knowledge that I was called of the Lord never left me. From that day I knew that I would enter the ministry and I never once wavered from that course. I knew also that the day would come when he would use me in a prophetic ministry. Two years later I began preaching in the village Methodist churches around the area where we lived. In less than two years, whilst still a sixteen-year-old schoolboy, I sat and passed the Methodist local preachers' exams.

Following national service, I entered college and received a highly liberal theological education. I went into college a simple Bible-believing Christian and, by the end of the first year, I had had the intensely painful experience of having my faith shot to pieces as the Bible was systematically ripped apart by sterile academic biblical criticism. Somehow I survived four years at university, pursuing a divinity degree and an ordination course. During this time I began to develop an intense interest in social and political affairs, probably in part as a reaction against the growing sense of disappointment and bewilderment at my theological education but also as a conscious response to the sense of prophetic calling that never left me. I went on to the London School of Economics to read Sociology and, in a determination to make myself academically competent, acquired a number of degrees.

A period in the pastoral ministry took me into the field of race relations which I pursued with crusading zeal, believing at that time that this was the sphere into which the Lord had called me and through which he would work out the prophetic ministry to which I was called. During the 1960s I wrote a number of books, became an adviser to the Home Office on race relations, visited the West Indies on behalf of the British Council of Churches and took part in more than a hundred radio and TV programmes, including weekly broadcasts to the Caribbean. There followed a period of university lecturing in Sociology, overlapping with a period of mission work in the East End of London.

The move from a preoccupation with race relations to

inner city mission was a time of intense spiritual growth for me in which some of my West Indian friends played a significant part. They were Pentecostals and I had never met Pentecostals before. In fact I had been taught in college that the gifts of the Spirit including the gift of tongues were a first-century phenomenon that died out with the early Church. Those who went in for that kind of thing today were merely displaying some kind of emotional gibberish. As a sociologist, I could account for it as a social phenomenon occurring among the deprived that gave religious status to those lacking in social status and a mode of expression to the inarticulate. As a liberal theologian, a radical academic and a neo-Marxist, I secretly despised all who claimed a personal experience of God. Anyone who spoke about 'the Lord' I cast as one of those queer irrational 'fundamentalists' or Bible-believers of whose existence I was dimly aware but with whom I never had any personal dealings.

My frequent visits to the homes of my black Pentecostal friends began to make a deep impression upon me. They always talked about 'the Lord' and they never let me leave without praying with me. This contrasted vividly with my visits to my white Christian friends and church members, when we talked about football, the economy or matters concerning the fellowship life of the church. As a pastor, I rarely prayed with people – if I did, they might think they were ill. If they were ill, I had to be careful or they might think they were dying! When my black Christian friends prayed they seemed to open the very windows of heaven and to talk to Jesus as though they actually knew him and as though he was in the room with them. Theirs was a powerful witness. Secretly, I had to admit that despite all my learning they knew God in a way that I didn't. And I was supposed to be the one with the prophetic ministry! It was ironic. They were a constant irritant in my spiritual life that I found profoundly disturbing.

The day came when I made a disastrous speech on 'The Sociology of the Family in Modern Britain' in the presence of seven hundred staff and students in Birmingham

University. They were too polite to boo me from the stage but I knew I deserved it! I had tried to say something with some Gospel in it and had only achieved some weak moralizing. For the first time in my life I tasted the bitterness of failure. I had always succeeded (at least, in my own eyes!) in anything that I undertook.

The Lord used that experience of personal failure to break the pride and self-will that were the real spiritual barriers in my life. I had to admit that the central dynamic in my life was 'self'. I didn't have any Gospel to give because I was walking in my own strength. The bitterness of that experience drove me in penitence before the Lord, submitting in a way that I had not done since my conversion and my teenage years of non-academic simplicity. The second line of the little chorus 'Spirit of the living God fall afresh on me' came true in my life. 'Break me, melt me, mould me, fill me . . .' Having fought a long and hard rear-guard action I was broken in spirit. God had melted the hardness of my heart and he began to mould me into the stature of a man in Christ Jesus and to fill me with his Spirit.

The difference in my ministry was radical. But even more so was the change in my spiritual life. I began to read the Bible in a new way. It was not simply that mentally I allowed the 'marginal redactions' to slip back into the text; neither was it simply that the problems of authorship and biblical criticism faded in importance; but rather, for the first time since the pre-college days of my theological innocence, I began to read the Bible as the word of the living God. It not only had a new authority, but a new power in my life.

From rediscovering the lordship of Jesus in my own life and discovering the power of the Holy Spirit for the first time, I began to discover God's overruling authority in all things. For several years I interpreted my prophetic calling in terms of inner city ministry and again threw myself into this with a crusading zeal.

It was at this point that we moved into the East End and began a period of ministry that brought intense joy and fulfilment as well as intense pain and anxiety. My wife entered fully into this ministry as she also began to move in the things of the Spirit and we saw God doing amazing things around us. We founded a faith ministry, 'The Renewal Programme', that brought together a team of committed Christians working with churches of different denominations in an area where the traditional churches had been declining for many years.

The work rapidly grew to the largest urban mission organization in the country, with a full-time staff of twenty-two and a great many more part-time and voluntary workers. Financially too the Lord opened the windows of heaven to us as we grew from nothing to an income of more than £100,000 a year in five years. This, in the 1970s, was a lot of money.

The ministry had its pain and sorrow as well, particularly as we saw the difficulties faced by our three children growing up in an area with every kind of social tension. We continually lifted them before the Lord and often cried to him over the problems they were facing, particularly in their education. It was a time of constant breaking and learning to trust and to depend upon the love of God. Then, quite unexpectedly, the invitation came to a position of national leadership in evangelism.

CHAPTER FOUR

Power and Direction

Leaving the East End which we dearly loved, and where we had seen dead churches come alive, individual lives changed and many wonderful signs of blessing upon our ministry, was a traumatic experience for both my wife and myself. We both left the people and the area we loved with a strong sense of bereavement. Yet we knew for certain that we were being obedient to God despite our personal grief. There were too many signs for us to dare to ignore them.

I had been receiving indications for some time that the day was drawing near when I would be brought into a wider sphere of ministry. My years of service in the inner city were part of God's essential preparation in my life. Even my strange academic background with its mixture of theology and sociology had prepared me for the task that lay ahead. I had learned to understand and to experience at first hand the great social issues in the most deprived sectors of society. For years I had lived among the tensions those issues generated. I had learned to survive through violence and riots. But above all I had grown to love and identify with the people amongst whom I lived and worked. I had an over-flowing compassion for those caught up in the network of violence both as aggressors and as the victims of violence. I understood, even though I could not condone the outcome, the fears and frustrations that led to aggression. I understood the hopelessness and despair that led many to give up the un-equal struggle and some even to the extremities of suicide.

I never forgot the young man I met in the early days of my ministry. He was lying in a hospital bed after an unsuccessful suicide attempt, having thrown himself in front of a train. He had only succeeded in getting both his legs cut off. He was one of life's failures. He couldn't even successfully commit suicide. He hadn't solved any of the problems that had driven him to despair, and at twenty-one he had to face the rest of his life as a legless cripple.

That young man seemed to me to be a parable of our world without Christ. Our politicians, diplomats, economists and social planners stumble from one expedient to the next. In the East End of London we had seen it all in microcosm; man's attempts to deal with his own social blunders in his own strength. We had seen the erection of huge tower blocks to replace the slum houses in urban renewal programmes, but they had only succeeded in creating a whole new set of social and personal problems. Community was smashed as people were stacked up into the sky and left isolated and lonely. The poverty areas of yesterday became the social disaster areas of more affluent days. Then came the attempt to solve the new set of problems by pouring in social workers and welfare programmes that increased the dependency of families and individuals who were already giving up the struggle. When will we learn to seek the Lord for his wisdom in planning our cities? When will we learn that love and justice, compassion and righteousness are all the ways of the Lord? When will we learn that only in his ways can we find life and peace and fulfilment? When will we learn?

Although the move from the East End was so painful as we broke the ties with those who had given us close prayer support and stood by us whenever the battle was hottest, I had the strong sense that each part of my life had been a preparation for whatever lay ahead. Yet I felt inadequate and unsure of the way ahead. I had no experience of large-scale evangelism and all my ministry had been within inner city working class communities. The national work I was entering was very different and I felt ill equipped for its demands.

After a few months of struggling with my new responsibilities I went away alone to my parents' cottage in rural Sussex. I spent a night in prayer, confessing my inadequacy and begging the Lord for a fresh anointing of his

Spirit to give me power and direction for whatever new ministry he had for me. Halfway through the following day, I entered into an intense spiritual experience whereby I found myself caught up into the presence of the living God.

The experience of that day has never left me. It changed the course of my life and drew me into a new relationship with God – a relationship of which I am constantly aware, day and night.

This experience took place early in 1979 and I have never spoken of it in public until now. The experience was in three parts. The first was a personal commissioning, the second was a message to the churches, and the third a message to the nations. As soon as possible afterwards I recorded the experience, reliving each detail vividly in order to preserve as accurate an account as possible. This has been transcribed and I print it below almost verbatim. The experience followed a time of praying and praising in the Spirit which brought with it a deep sense of peace and resting in God:

'A most glorious sense of joy now came to me that mingled with the peace that had already come. It was a mixture of joy and peace that brought me sinking to the floor and I just lay there and enjoyed his presence. I knew what Augustine meant, that the whole purpose of our human life is to know God and to enjoy him for ever. I felt that I had never enjoyed him like this in my life before and I wanted to go on enjoying him for ever and ever. It was more exquisite and more marvellous than anything I had ever experienced before. I began again to praise him in the Spirit and to thank him, and the words poured off my lips. I had never praised him with such sweet reality in all my days. It was as though it was his Spirit within me praying. The words were not my own, they were truly his because I was in unity with him. For these brief moments I was utterly and completely his because I had been emptied of self and filled with his presence, the reality of his love and his overwhelming power. It was his Spirit within me communicating with the Godhead. I was linked with God, I belonged to him, utterly and completely. He had all of me.

'I lay there for some time, praising him, I have no idea for how long, just quietly enjoying his presence and experiencing the sweet one-ness of resting in him, and gradually I found myself beginning to cry; it wasn't just tears of joy but I was beginning now to cry in the Spirit. I didn't know why. I was more and more puzzled. "Why, Lord, why am I crying now when I am so happy? Why should I be sad?"'

'My crying turned into sobs and I felt my body beginning to heave; I couldn't understand it and I was frightened and yet I knew that I couldn't stop it, that it was of the Lord. This time my tears were not tears of penitence, as they had been earlier in the day, but I knew that the Lord was pushing me towards some new experience and I was frightened and I began to say, "No, Lord, no, Lord, spare me". I couldn't think why I was saying this because I knew he was with me and I belonged to him. I couldn't understand why I was afraid, and in that moment, I seemed to be caught away to the Garden of Gethsemane on the night in which the Lord was betrayed and for some reason I couldn't understand, I began saying words similar to those that Jesus had said, "Lord, take this cup away from me. No, Lord, no, Lord, don't let me drink it. Keep it away from me. Keep it away from me." Within moments I found myself in the other part of the garden where there was a tomb and I could see the dark emptiness inside the tomb and the stone rolled away and I thought I was going to see Jesus.

'I could see a light but I couldn't see his face, but I knew it was his presence and I could feel his arms outstretched towards me and I could experience his presence growing in a greater and greater reality. He was coming towards me and I was going towards him. I was getting nearer and nearer to the tomb and I knew that he was going to say something to me and to do something in my life.

'The fear went from me then but my heaving sobs turned into a writhing movement of my body. My arms were suddenly flung out by my side and my whole body began to writhe and twist and I was in pain, terrible pain. Suddenly the pain intensified in my hands and shot up my arms and went piercing right through my body, and my body seemed to be torn apart. There was the most fearful pain in my stomach and I shook and writhed and moaned and begged the Lord not to go on with it and I found myself saying, "I'm being crucified with Christ. O Lord, O Lord, take this away from me." And I felt a terrible pain in my lips. My mouth was dry and my lips were parched and hard and the verses of Isaiah 6 ran through my mind:

"Woe to me!" I cried. "I am ruined! For I am a man of unclean lips, and I live among a people of unclean lips, and my eyes have seen the king, the Lord Almighty."

Then one of the seraphs flew to me with a live coal in his hand, which he had taken with tongs from the altar. With it he touched my mouth and said, "See, this has touched your lips; your guilt is taken away and your sin atoned for."

Then I heard the voice of the Lord saying, "Whom shall I send? And who will go for us?"

And I said, "Here am I. Send me!"   (Isaiah 6:5–8)

'I felt a burning sensation on my lips as though a live coal had touched them. I knew that the Lord was cleansing me of my sins and that he was commissioning me and laying upon me the mantle of the prophet.

'The pain still shook my body, but gradually it diminished and I knew that the Lord was giving me a message that he had taken me from my mother's womb and called me to be his servant and that, through me, he would bring his word to the nations. I no longer protested but gradually I grew calmer and the pain diminished and I sank back again and lay there exhausted.

'I don't know how long I lay there but the peace and the sense of joy returned and I simply lay there and enjoyed the presence of God. But it was not for long. Soon I felt myself crying again and my crying turned into the same sobs and the sobs grew louder and heavier and more uncontrollable. I knew that the Spirit of the Lord was coming upon me again and I felt afraid in the same way as before, and I began to resist him. But I knew that it was inevitable and my body began to be shaken and as I writhed again, the pains came again. They intensified and then came the same sudden terrible piercing pain in my hands, the pain that shot up my arms and raged through my body and racked me and tore me apart. I began to say, "No, Lord, no, Lord, no, no, no, I don't want it. Take it away from me, Lord." Then I found myself saying, "This is for my Church, this is the message for the Church." I heard his voice saying through my lips, "You must repent. You must be broken. You must come to penitence. There will be tears. There will be brokenness, but there will be much rejoicing and blessing. This is the way of renewal. This is the renewal of the Lord. It will come upon my Church. My Church shall be cleansed. My Church shall be my servant. My Church shall be renewed and be my servant to the nations."

'Whilst I was saying this, there came to my mind a picture of a church. I could see inside. The congregation was seated. I saw the people getting up out of their seats and going forward with tears in their eyes and crying before the Lord. I knew there was going to be brokenness and penitence before the Lord would return and I knew that this was something that only God could do.

'The searing pain was still running through my body and as the tears streamed down my face I felt that my tears were mingling with the tears of the people and I began to say to the Lord, "What shall I do, Lord? What shall I do?" And I knew that he was saying to me, "Tell my people to repent. There is nothing more that you can do to bring this people to me, but I will do it. Only I can do it. Through brokenness my people will return to me." I heard him saying, "I, if I be lifted up will draw all men unto me." And I knew that the only thing I had to do was to glorify Christ, to give him the glory. I simply had to pray that God would be glorified, that the presence of Christ would be lifted up among his people. Then he would do his work in their hearts and bring renewal to his body.

'The peace began to return to me. The pain subsided and I sank back exhausted and began to enjoy again the sweet peace and joy of the beauty of his presence.

'How long I remained like that I don't know but again I found myself beginning to cry and my crying became more and more heavy. The tears began to roll down my face and I had the feeling of fear grip my heart again. Again, I didn't understand this fear and began to talk to the Lord. "Remove this cup from me, Lord. Remove this cup from me. Don't let me have to go through this, Lord. Don't let me have to drink this cup. I cannot stand it, Lord." I began to pray and to pray and to beg and implore him not to take me through this because I knew that this was going to be the worst of all.

'The third experience was coming upon me and I knew that it was going to be the most painful and terrifying of all. As the climax built up my sobs became uncontrollable and I was gripped by the inevitableness of it all and I knew that I had just got to go through it. Again, my body began to hurt all over and to writhe and the pain began again in my hands and tore up through my arms, and my body was racked. I knew that I was entering into the fellowship of his sufferings and the words came pouring out of my lips. "O Lord, O Lord, no, no," I was saying, "O God, no."

'I began to see the most terrifying vision. "O Lord," I said. "No, God, I can't bear to see it." And I heard the voice of the Lord saying, "This is the message. This is for the nations. This is for the nations." And my lips were speaking the words, "This is for the nations." And I saw the most fearful destruction coming upon the land. I saw a dark cloud, like the mushroom cloud of a great big explosion, a terrifying, whirling wind that was coming down out of the skies and was spinning so fast that it seemed to be rising, then falling, and to be sucking up and smashing down and destroying. I saw the dust and the clouds of destruction sweeping across the earth, destroying, destroying everything that was swept up.

'As it passed through the land I saw people, bodies whirling, being flung here and there and everywhere and being shattered to pieces as they were caught up in the terrifying dark clouds of destruction. And I began to cry aloud as my body was racked in this terrible enormity of pain and I shouted to God. "Spare them! Spare them! O God, stop it, Lord. Stop it! Don't let it happen! Stop it now, Lord, before it goes any further. It's not fair, Lord! It's not fair! Don't bring this upon them, God. They're not all evil. Spare them, Lord, it's not fair."

'And even then at that moment I began to see the other side of the vision. The dark cloud faded into a light that was on the left hand side of the vision and with my right eye it seemed I could still see the clouds of destruction sweeping with terrifying fury through the land. And now my attention was focused through my left eye upon the light and I could see the light, as it were, breaking through the clouds. It seemed as though I was there myself and I was looking up into the sky and it was the very opening of heaven. I said, "O God, this is beautiful. It's wonderful. Your light is streaming down and there's such a great and powerful light. Its brilliance I have never seen before or could possibly imagine."

'There was light too upon the earth but it was not so powerful and I could see it was streaming up as well as the light that was streaming down. But the light that was streaming up was much weaker and was almost a pale reflection of the light that was coming down. I could see the two sources of light merge and become one and joined and I experienced a great joy even through the pain and suffering that was still running through my body.

'I could feel the tingling excitement of joy. The pain that was running through my arms seemed to turn to a new sweetness of suffering and I could see the very angels of heaven, the very light of the presence of God streaming upon the earth and it seemed there was a movement coming down and my lips were saying, "This is the Church triumphant coming upon the land." And I could see the people on earth being caught up and I knew that the saints of the Lord were being caught up to join the people of God who were with him in his presence and were enjoying him for ever to all eternity. There was a great link-up between heaven and earth and I could feel my lips saying, "This is the Church triumphant joining with the Church militant. The two are one! Praise the Lord!" And I could feel the glory of his presence shining round about and as I gave glory to God so the pain in my body diminished and the sweet joy of his presence was such an overwhelming, glowing reality that as the vision was still there before my eyes, I began to sink back again and the pain grew less in my arms and in my stomach. The great heaving painful sighs in my chest grew less and less.

'The darker side of the vision that I could still see there seemed to be overshadowed and overruled and almost to fade into the background through the wonderful reality of the vision in my left eye.

'"O Lord," I said, "how beautiful and how wonderful is your presence." My lips began to say, "This is the message to the nations. This is my word." As I began to say this and was still enjoying the sweetness of the presence of the Lord, I began to cry slightly and to say, "No, Lord. No, Lord. No. Take away this message. Don't let me have to give this, Lord. I know that they will laugh at me and jeer. They won't believe me, Lord. They won't believe me. I shall be scorned and rejected." I could feel the pain and suffering of that but it was all part of the same experience. The pain in my body was still growing less, but it was just the fear that was in my heart.

'As I said these words I just cried before the Lord and my head shook and I was still saying, "No, Lord. I can't bear it. I can't give this message." He said to me, "You shall. It will not be you. This is my word." And I heard him say, "My grace is sufficient for you. You shall be my messenger to the nations. My strength is all you need."

'I gradually subsided and lay there, enjoying the sweetness of his presence. The vision faded from my sight and I knew there would be no more. This was the end.'

*

Two days later I had a private meeting in London with my

personal support group. They were Canon Harry Sutton of St Paul's, Portman Square, the Reverend Gilbert Kirby, Principal of London Bible College, and Mr Gordon Landreth, General Secretary of the Evangelical Alliance. They graciously listened to me relive the entire experience with each detail of the vision. They questioned me and prayed with me at some length. Then each affirmed his conviction that God had spoken to me, that this vision was of the Lord. We all four agreed that we would say nothing to anyone concerning this and that in his own time God would make it clear to me what he wished me to do. Three months later I wrote *Towards the Dawn*, which was a message especially for Britain. Then the following year I began work on *The Day Comes*, which looked at the international scene and applied the vision of Isaiah chapters 24–27 to the nations of the contemporary world.

Privately I hoped that I would never have to reveal my vision or to speak of the things God had been saying to me over a number of years. It was easy to write analytically as I did in *Towards the Dawn* and in *The Day Comes*. All my previous books had been in this style. It suited me not only academically but emotionally as well. I do not find it easy to express myself emotionally. Although I've moved in charismatic renewal circles for quite a number of years it was a long time before I could raise my hands with any real freedom and I still have never danced before the Lord and probably never will, except within my spirit! Fortunately I know that he understands, because he made me the way I am. He knows the love I have for him within my heart.

I am saying all this to underline how difficult it has been for me to publish the contents of this chapter. I am not easily moved to tears and to describe an intensely personal experience in which I cried before the Lord and to make the details public has been an incredibly difficult decision. I only do so in absolute obedience to the Spirit's direction.

Rationally, too, it has not been easy to cope with the things God has been saying to me. Academically my strongly rationalistic background makes it difficult to conceive that

God communicates with us by revelation. It needed the blinding impact of the experience I've just described to convince me of the reality of God's present communication that has since opened the way for him to speak to me on many more occasions and to lead me into a new phase of ministry.

Taking up this new phase of ministry was an act of faith as well as obedience. It meant leaving the security of employment as well as the status of a national office. With no salary, my wife in full-time unpaid ministry, and with two children still dependent upon us it meant looking to the Lord for everything. I had to be free from organizational responsibilities, from committees, councils, reports and such things in order to have time to write and to speak wherever the opportunity is given to bring the message. I know what it is to exercise a faith ministry and to trust him in everything, even for our daily bread.

There have been several occasions during the past two years when, with all our savings gone, we have literally not had the money to buy food. But he has always supplied and put a new song of praise and thanksgiving upon our lips as we have rejoiced in his perfect timing and the wonder of his love that knows no bounds. We have often been strengthened and encouraged by the promise God gave to Joshua when he undertook the seemingly impossible task of leading Israel across Jordan into Canaan. Humanly speaking the man was totally inadequate for the immense responsibilities laid upon him. But God said,

> As I was with Moses so I will be with you; I will never leave you or forsake you. Be strong and courageous.
>
> (Joshua 1:5 and 6)

That phrase 'Be strong and courageous' is repeated four times in chapter one. God was emphasizing the need for complete trust and obedience with the assurance of his abiding presence.

Be strong and courageous. Do not be terrified; do not be discouraged for the Lord your God will be with you wherever you go.   (Joshua 1:9)

Whenever God calls to a task HE supplies the enabling!

CHAPTER FIVE

Future Events

God is speaking to us afresh of his love and his good purposes for mankind. He is doing this to prepare the way for us to hear and receive the message concerning the great dangers facing mankind. I believe that God is giving us forewarning that in the lifetime of the present generation of children judgement will come upon our civilization. Millions of mankind will be annihilated in a nuclear holocaust, unless the nations turn away from their present course.

It is not God's will that this should happen. Indeed, God is urgently communicating with us to warn us of the incredible danger we are in and to show that there is another way. He has good plans for us. His purposes for mankind are for good and not for evil. He is longing to save us from the consequences of our own evil actions and desires. His way of salvation is plain. It is the only way: full repentance and the turning of his people to him in love and trust to seek his way.

It is not inevitable that destruction will come upon the world, and it is not too late to turn to God and be saved. But it will be inevitable, absolutely inevitable, if the nations continue on their present course. The choice is ours! We choose either life or death!

God is longing to lead the nations in the path of peace, but he will have to act if we continue to pursue the road that leads to destruction and death. Of course God maintains his sovereign control in that he already knows the choice we will make, for he is the God of the future as well as the God of history, holding the nations in his hands as a drop in a bucket. He will work out his purposes. His glory will be seen and his reign upon earth established, even if it has to be through the terrible breaking of the nations and the suffering and death that will come upon millions of men, women and children whom he made and whom he loves.

Nevertheless, the choice is a free one. God is holding out life towards us while the enemy is driving us towards death and destruction. He is urgently reminding us of his great and limitless love. As the father of that stricken child sliding down the snowy mountainside at Adelboden rushed to save her, so God is reaching out to save mankind in this generation. If we do not heed him – if we do not allow him to pluck us out of the path of destruction and to pick us up into his loving arms – if we ignore him and dash past him he will go over the precipice with us to pick up the shattered remnant of mankind from the rocks below. There will come a time of restoration. For he is the God of resurrection, of life and not death; he only can lead us in the way everlasting.

He is calling out to us today with the same choice that he offered to the people of Jerusalem in the days when the very existence of that city was threatened by the oncoming Chaldean armies. This is how Jeremiah announced the choice to the house of Judah:

> If at any time I announce that a nation or kingdom is to be uprooted, torn down and destroyed, and if that nation I warned repents of its evil, then I will relent and not inflict on it the disaster I had planned. And if at another time I announce that a nation or kingdom is to be built up and planted, and if it does evil in my sight and does not obey me, then I will reconsider the good I had intended to do for it.
>
> Now therefore say to the people of Judah and those living in Jerusalem, 'This is what the Lord says: Look! I am preparing a disaster for you and devising a plan against you. So turn from your evil ways, each one of you, and reform your ways and your actions.' But they will reply, 'It's no use. We will continue with our own plans; each of us will follow the stubbornness of his evil heart.'
>
> (Jeremiah 18:7–12)

That was precisely what the people of Jerusalem did under their weak and corrupt political and religious leaders; and their behaviour was compounded by the general faithlessness of their generation. The result was inevitable. Nebuchadnezzar's armies arrived and surrounded the city. There was no miracle of deliverance because there was no expectation or trust in God. There was a long siege and finally the city walls were broken, the ravaging hordes of barbarism were let loose upon the populace and after the slaughter the city was destroyed. It is a terrible picture of the consequences of the failure to heed the warnings of impending disaster which God sends to his people.

The nations of the world today are not in the same covenant relationship with the Lord that at one time covered Israel and Judah. Nevertheless God has called a new people into being throughout the world. They are a people who are a nation among the nations, those who love and acknowledge Jesus as Lord and Saviour. To them God is addressing his words today and to them he is looking to witness to their own nations. It is they whom he is holding responsible, each for his own nation. The people of the new covenant who are to be found in every nation of the world are the watchmen to whom God is appealing and through whom he is witnessing to the whole family of mankind.

In later chapters we shall look at this witness and see what God requires of his people. First it is necessary to look at the path the nations of the world are taking, to note the direction and destination so that we may know what it is we are witnessing against. God is sending us this foreknowledge of future events so that the children of light may be aware of the enemy's moves and may witness effectively to the children of darkness. God is longing for them to turn away from the deeds of darkness and to come into his light. It is not his wish that one of his children should perish but that the whole family of mankind may be saved. This is the great and good purpose of God.

We are moving inexorably into the last days of this present

age and I believe that God is revealing to us a possible pattern of future events. Before we outline these it is necessary firmly to state two things. First, when we speak of 'the end of the age' we are not talking of the end of the world. There are many ages in past world history. They can be any length of time from a few decades to a thousand years or more. An age, in biblical terms, is simply a period of time, of any duration, marking a phase in the relationship between God and his people.

In biblical terms, it was the end of the age when the period of the Judges gave way to the beginning of the monarchy. It was the end of another age when the kingdom divided. It was the end of the age for Israel, the northern kingdom, when Samaria fell in 722 BC. It was the end of the age for Judah, the southern kingdom, when Jerusalem was destroyed in 587 BC. It was the end of the next age when Jerusalem was destroyed again in AD 70 by the Romans as Jesus had prophesied, and the people of Judea were scattered throughout the nations.

They will fall by the sword and will be taken prisoners to all the nations. Jerusalem will be trampled on by the Gentiles until the times of the Gentiles are fulfilled.

(Luke 21:24)

It was the beginning of the end of the age for the Jews when they rejected Jesus the Messiah and crucified him, although it was some forty years later that Jerusalem fell to the Roman general Titus and the last days of the old age were finally completed. Meanwhile the new age, the age of the Holy Spirit, had already dawned. It began with the day of Pentecost and the outpouring of the Holy Spirit upon the disciples that filled Jerusalem with the knowledge of the resurrection of Jesus and gave life and hope to thousands.

Just as there was an overlap period in New Testament times with the dying of the old age and the rising of the new age, so today we are witnessing a change-over period. 'The times of the Gentiles' are already fulfilled. They have been fulfilled in our own lifetime with the re-establishment of the State of Israel on the ancient soil of the promised land and the restoration of Jerusalem into its hands. But the end of this age is not yet complete. We are living in the last days.

The second thing to be said with equal firmness is that we are not predicting dates and times! Jesus warned very clearly against such usurping of the Father's authority. He told his own disciples, when they asked questions about the timing of future events, 'It is not for you to know the times or dates the Father has set by his own authority' (Acts 1:7). Yet at the same time he does instruct us to be a watching, praying people, with the ability to discern the signs of the times. He rebuked the Pharisees, who were able to look up into the sky and forecast the weather but lacked the eyes of spiritual discernment to enable them to interpret rightly the signs of the times. God wants his people to be able to discern these 'signs of the times' in order to be aware of what he is doing and what he is calling his children to do at any particular time. This discernment is essential today; the days in which we live are critical.

In days of crisis God raises up prophets to speak to his people, to give them forewarning of coming events, or of impending danger. He does this not simply for their own sake, or for their own protection, but to give them guidance and direction for the action they should take and the leadership they should exercise in their generation. God has declared, 'Surely the sovereign Lord does nothing without revealing his plan to his servants, the prophets' (Amos 3:7). I believe the following paragraphs represent the pattern of events that will take place if the nations continue on their present course.

There will be a steady increase in dissolute lifestyles, an increase in competitiveness and selfishness caused by a growing spirit of materialism.

The stability of family life will continue to decline. Children will become increasingly neglected and insecure, lacking love and a stable home life. The practice of abortion and euthanasia will become widespread. Sexual deviance will increase; homosexuality will be openly practised and condoned even by those in positions of high authority.

Lawlessness and violence will increase in cities throughout the world; political uncertainty will also increase. Throughout the Western world there will be indecisive government and political instability. This will both be the result of, and contribute towards, massive social and economic problems.

The growth of cities throughout the world, especially in the developing nations, will increase worldwide instability. The social and moral diseases of the old nations will quickly spread to the newer nations with their rapidly expanding populations and vast unemployment.

International terrorist movements, well organized and armed, will gain ascendancy. New forms of terrorism will add to the political uncertainty of many nations; assassinations will remove experienced leadership.

Urban warfare will afflict many great cities. The forces of law and order will not be able to deal with the widespread disorder that will shake the stability of the nations.

There will be revolutions and attempted revolutions; including a great upheaval in southern Africa. This will have worldwide effects, especially in the economic sphere. The banking systems of the Western world will be in disarray. The major world currencies will all be shaken.

Then, out of the worldwide political and economic chaos there will arise new orders of political oppression. Both the Eastern and the Western worlds will be led by leaders invested with massive political power. Totalitarian government in the East will be more repressive than anything so far known within the Communist world. Similarly in the West the nations will willingly accept a strong leader who will purport to lead them as an economic saviour into more prosperous times. Those prosperous economic times will in fact begin and the economically fruitful policies of the Western world leader will increase his power. Men will willingly follow him but in the end he will lead them to destruction.

There will be widespread persecution of Christians in many lands. Christians will be blamed for many of the world's troubles and they will be hated among the nations. Many will fall away from the faith, and among those who remain faithful there will be many martyrs.

A general increase in tension between the nations, particularly among the smaller nations of the world, will accompany the worldwide decline in natural mineral resources. The lack of natural resources, particularly oil and basic minerals, will severely restrict the economies of the smaller nations who lack the political and military muscle to compete for their needs in a competitive world. The tension among these smaller nations, although it will be regarded as insignificant by the larger nations, in fact poses the greatest threat to world stability and peace. Many of these smaller nations will be armed with the most incredible weapons of destruction.

The final conflict will begin through a clash of the smaller nations in the Middle East. The larger nations will be drawn in, resulting in the eventual clash between the super-powers and the all-out exchange of strategic nuclear weapons. This in turn will set off a chain reaction of destruction around the world that could affect all life upon this planet.

I believe that if the chain of events continues to this point God will intervene. In his own perfect timing he will subdue the nations. He will establish his own authority over the nations and will be seen in his power and glory by the remnant of mankind. Men of all nations will acknowledge him as King of kings and Lord of lords, and in the Name of Jesus every knee will bow. I believe this to be a right interpretation of scripture. It may be that God will intervene through the second coming of our Lord but I have refrained from offering an opinion on this. We are meant to be a people who live in expectation not in speculation!

It is my firm conviction that God will not allow men to destroy the world that is the creation of his own hands and that he saw was good. Yet the whole history of God's dealing with his people shows that he will not protect an unholy generation. He actively allows judgement to come upon them through their enemies. Then he steps in to bring restoration and to rebuild the life of future generations through a purged remnant. God did not even save Jersualem from destruction during the time of Jeremiah when a rebellious generation refused to hear and to heed his word. Neither did he save Jerusalem from destruction during the Roman occupation after the nation had rejected and crucified his son.

The sequence of future world events that I have offered above has been borne out of those things that God has shown to me in recent years and of the passages of scripture that relate to the times in which we live.

I can never anticipate when God is going to speak to me. Neither can I predict what he will say. There are long periods when I hear nothing. Sometimes he will speak through an event such as the fall of the child in the Swiss Alps which is recorded at the beginning of this book. At other times he will bring a picture into my mind and then interpret it. Sometimes he speaks through a period of prolonged prayer and meditation. It is at such times, when the Spirit of the Lord comes upon me, that I have learned to have a pen and paper nearby to write down the words as they come to me.

For those who are not used to handling prophecy I should explain that when the Hand of the Lord comes upon me and I write under the direction of the Spirit it is quite different from ordinary writing where I am thinking at least two or three sentences ahead. Prophecy is entirely different. When I begin to write I have no idea what will be set down. Once it is written I never alter a word. I am often surprised at the words that come. Sometimes I even find myself arguing with the Lord, and that is reflected in what I write. But the words don't just appear. I am most certainly not in a trance! Prophecy has nothing whatever to do with spiritism. When the Hand of the Lord comes upon me I am thinking quite clearly, but I am not aware of what the next sentence will be. I simply write down the words as they come into my mind. I am the recorder, the messenger, not the author as I am when I write a book, or compose an essay.

Prophecy is tested through prayer and through the witness of the Holy Spirit within you. A genuine prophecy will never contradict scripture. It will always glorify Christ Jesus as Lord and Saviour. It will usually be confirmed through what God is saying to other prophets. It must be accompanied by confirming signs in the prophet's own life, as a man of God walking in a right relationship with the Lord. The final test, of course, lies in the fulfilment of the prophecy.

These are days when the enemy is at work among us. False prophecy abounds and Christians need to beware of accepting uncritically any word that purports to be from God. That includes what is written in this book. There are no exceptions outside the Bible. But as Paul says, 'Do not put out the Spirit's fire; do not treat prophecies with contempt. Test everything. Hold on to the good. Avoid every kind of evil' (1 Thessalonians 5:19-22). God has spoken to me many times in recent years and I have stored up the words until I receive clear instructions to release them. That release has been given for one of those prophecies which I print below word for word so that Christians who are exercising the gifts of the Spirit can test it.

I find God speaks to me in the ordinary everyday language with which I am familiar. He does not speak to me in ancient Hebrew or in ancient English; there is no 'thus says the Lord' in it. If the words truly are from God, as I believe them to be, Christians will not need any familiar phrases to convince them. They will know if God is speaking to them. That is the ministry of the Holy Spirit.

This particular word flowed straight out of a time of praise and adoration which is reflected in the opening paragraph.

Praise be to you O God for you alone are God of all creation. To you alone belongs all honour and glory, for you stretched out the heavens and placed the planets in their orbits. You created the ends of the universe. Your wisdom and might, majesty and power, are beyond the wit of man to comprehend. Yet you have taught us to call you Father, you have made man but a little lower than the angels. You are God and there is no other. Praise your great and glorious name.

Tell the nations of the West that calamity is coming upon them. Woe to you proud nations who devour the produce of the land as though you were the last generation of men. You who have no concern for others who say, 'the earth is ours and not God's', you shall be brought low. In the day of my wrath you cannot stand. It will blow like a whirlwind across the seas and the land shall be withered and dried up. The nations will be shaken, none can survive unscathed.

I am hardening men's hearts so that hearing they do not hear and seeing they do not see lest they turn and repent and delay my hand of judgement. I long to see my people turn to me but they are a rebellious generation and will not heed my word. They are so blind they do not see the signs I have sent them. The nations will be purged, they shall be clean. They shall stand before me naked and unashamed when the dross is purged and they turn to me and glorify my name.

Why Lord, what have we done? Why will judgement come upon the West? Because though you have my word you do not heed it. Though you proclaim my word you do not believe it. Though you declare my word you do not live it. You are not living stones, you are dead stones – a dead memorial that is lifeless and powerless – not a living witness that is honouring to my name.

Look to yourselves, you people who claim my name, you who say 'We are of Christ'. There is corruption and evil among you. You are a faithless generation. You are indistinguishable from the world. Your families are in disarray, your households are disorderly, your marriages are unfaithful. Your leaders are unbelievers and you are like father, like sons. You are a faithless generation and you shall not see my Face until you are purified and refined.

Yet I plead with you my children. It is not my will that destruction shall come upon the earth. Trust me. Turn to me. Hear me. Look to me and be saved. Only in me is there salvation. Only I can stop the nations running to the pit. Only I can save them from the valley of Jehoshaphat. It is the valley of death. But I am the God of life and I long to see light and life among the nations.

I gave my people as a light to the Gentiles and I gave my Son for the life of the world. What more can I do for you, rebellious children? Can you not see the path you are treading only has one end?

There is yet hope. Turn to me, ends of the earth. Let the people hear. Let the nations hear the trumpet of their God. Sound the call to engage the enemy. Rise up, people of God, you who claim the name of Jesus as Saviour, rise up and proclaim him in the hearing of the nations. Let all people hear our God! Let the word of the Lord sound among the nations! Proclaim his salvation in the ears of the leaders of the people. Let them hear and turn to their God and say, 'We will return to Zion, to the city of our God. We will exalt his Name and seek his face that his will may be done on earth and his Name may be glorified for ever and ever.'

I believe that God is revealing to us the possible future pattern of events, not because it is inevitable, but because he is warning us of the great danger facing us. At the same time he is re-emphasizing his great love for all his children and his great and good purposes for mankind. That is the major theme of his love. His warnings are part of that message of love.

God loves the whole family of man for we are all his

creation, and he has a special message of love for those who belong to him through the saving work of the Lord Jesus. To them he is addressing the appeal to turn to him in holiness and penitence, to love him and to trust him. Through them he is calling upon the nations of the world to repent. Through them he is bringing his word to a rebellious generation.

It is inevitable that temporal judgement will come upon the nations if they do not heed the word of the Lord and repent. God is making these things known now, beforehand, so that men may be given a further chance to review the consequences of their own actions and to see in stark reality the choice that is open to them. It is indeed the choice between the way of peace and life and the way of destruction and death.

God has not given us up. He is still fighting to save mankind. It is in fact a battle for the soul of the nations. In essence it is a spiritual battle. God is calling upon all his people to join the battle. He is sending out a call to arms. He is raising an army of the Spirit worldwide, a prophetic people to witness to the nations.

The first thing that God is calling upon his people to do is to recognize *the nature of the warfare*. The battle in which we are involved is spiritual warfare. The arms we need are not therefore the arms of flesh but the weapons of the Spirit.

In the next two chapters we shall be examining what God is doing throughout the world to mobilize his people to meet the emergency of the times in which we live. Despite the enormous threat and immense dangers to mankind, these are exciting days to be a Christian! God is at work! We belong to him whatever happens. The final victory is his! The outcome is assured, so too is our salvation. He has promised to abide with us for ever: 'Surely I will be with you always, even to the end of the age' (Matthew 28:20).

That is the solemn promise of Jesus the Son of God. In his word we may have absolute confidence. In his love we may have absolute trust. His is the victory! His is the kingdom, and the power, and the glory, for ever and ever. Amen!

CHAPTER SIX

Hezekiah's Revival

One of the ways in which God helps us to understand what he is doing today and what he requires of us his people is to remind us of what he has done in times past under similar circumstances. God has always used this method. Time and again he took the Israelites back to first base, reminding them of their spiritual heritage. He reminded them of the way he dealt with their forefathers, Abraham, Isaac and Jacob. Above all he reminded them time and again of his loving-kindness and compassion for Israel in the days of her suffering in Egypt; he reminded them that he had heard the cry of the people and become known to them as a great saving God through the deliverance of his people from Egypt.

God is reminding us today that his nature has not changed. He is still a God of compassion and loving-kindness, with a great desire to care for his people. His people today, those who are in a covenant relationship with him, are not just of one nation, stemming from one family, as in the days of ancient Israel. Although they are indeed one family, the people of God today, hundreds of millions throughout the world, are drawn from every race, nation, tribe and tongue – all who have accepted Jesus as Saviour and thereby entered into a new and right relationship with God our Father. It is essential that we understand clearly this basic New Testament declaration that all who accept Christ as Lord and Saviour become incorporated into the new Israel of God. They thus become the inheritors of the promises and the covenant. Peter sums this up powerfully when he declares:

But you are a chosen people, a royal priesthood, a holy nation, a people belonging to God, that you may declare the praises of him who called you out of darkness into his wonderful light. Once you were not a people, but now you are the people of God. (1 Peter 2:9 and 10)

That statement of Peter's was addressed to the whole Church, to both Jew and Gentile. Paul sees this as the great mystery of the Gospel that through Jesus God has 'destroyed the barrier, the dividing wall of hostility' (Ephesians 3:14) between Jew and Gentile.

His purpose was to create in himself one new man out of the two, thus making peace, and in this one body to reconcile both of them to God through the cross, by which he put to death their hostility. (Ephesians 2:15 and 16)

The outcome of this great work of reconciliation through which people of all nations are brought into union with God and with each other through Christ is that they become heirs to all the promises God has made to his people over many generations.

This mystery is that through the Gospel the Gentiles are heirs together with Israel, members together of one body, and sharers together in the promise in Christ Jesus.

(Ephesians 3:6)

There are no exact parallel circumstances to those facing mankind today. There never has been a time when the threat to the very existence of the whole of mankind has been as real as it is today. But there have been times in the history of the old Israel when there was a similar threat of annihilation building up against the nation. We can learn something of God's purposes and his ways of dealing with people in the time of great danger by studying what he did in those days.

Towards the end of the eighth century BC, when the Assyrian empire was at the height of its power, when the armies of Sargon and then Sennacherib marched victorious and all-conquering across every land in the Middle East, the tiny nation of Judah, God's people of the covenant, was in a state of internal chaos and disarray. The social, economic and political malaise of the nation was spiritual in essence. The worship of idols had been widely practised among the people for many years, but King Ahaz had given great encouragement to the idolators by his own evil practices. He practised all that was corrupt and detestable in the worship of the nations surrounding Judah, not refraining even from child sacrifice.

Ahaz encouraged homosexuality, Temple prostitution and even burnt his own son in an orgy of witchcraft and violence. He added to the spiritual plight of the nation by actively deterring all those who wished to worship the Lord and to remain pure in their spiritual lives and loyalty to God. He forbade the priests from teaching the people or offering worship to the Lord; towards the end of his life he actually closed the Temple, nailing up its doors so that no one could enter. Ahaz officially proscribed the worship of God throughout the land. He set up altars for idolatrous practices in every town and village throughout Judah and even placed idolatrous shrines on every street corner within the city of Jerusalem (2 Chronicles 28:24–25).

Family life was affected, loyalties were divided as spiritism and all manner of evil practices spread among the people. Immorality, injustice and violence characterized the social life of the nation. Political intrigue and corruption added to the general disarray – and all this at a time when on the international front there were gathering storm clouds that posed a threat to the survival and very existence of God's people as a nation.

The northern kingdom of Israel, with its capital in Samaria, had already fallen in the year 722 BC. The policy of the Assyrians, that had been begun by Tiglath-Pileser, was to extend their empire by incorporating one country after another in order to quell the possibility of rebellion by destroying both the national solidarity and the national identity of each conquered nation. They did this by uprooting whole communities in each of the lands their army overcame and transporting the people to other parts of the empire. They then transplanted Assyrian communities to live in the newly conquered lands, to intermarry, to change the culture and to promote the homogeneity of the entire empire.

With the fall of Israel it was clear to everyone in the southern kingdom that Judah was next in line for the Assyrian holocaust. And the nation was in a state of utter moral and spiritual disarray! Impoverished economically through unsuccessful wars with Syria and Israel, her army disorganized, her leadership dissolute and corrupt, her people lawless and violent, the plight of Judah appeared hopeless.

At the right moment God intervened. Ahaz, although still a comparatively young man, died. He was succeeded by his son Hezekiah, only twenty-five years old, but a God-fearing young man. He had been well taught; he loved the Lord with all his heart and trusted him completely. Clearly he hadn't got his love of the Lord from his father or sound teaching in the law from the priests, who had been banned by Ahaz. We can only assume that his mother, Abijah, loved the Lord and faithfully taught her son.

Hezekiah's first action when he became king was to re-open the Temple, reinstate the priests and re-establish true worship in the city of Jerusalem.

> In the first month of the first year of his reign, he opened the doors of the Temple of the Lord and repaired them. He brought in the priests and the Levites, assembled them in the square on the east side and said, 'Listen to me, Levites! Consecrate yourselves now and consecrate the Temple of the Lord, the God of your fathers. Remove all defilements from the sanctuary.'   (2 Chronicles 29:3–5)

The next thing Hezekiah did was to send out word to all Judah and to the fragmented communities of the scattered nation of Israel, still linked as they were by their common heritage in the Lord, calling them to Jerusalem to celebrate the Passover. This call was a considerable break with tradition since the Passover was always celebrated in the month of Abib, the first month of the year, as that was the month in which Israel had been brought out of slavery in Egypt. But Hezekiah was not going to be bound by tradition and thereby prevented from doing what was necessary in the life of the nation. This was an emergency. The first thing that was needed was to get the nation into a right relationship with God. After that he could begin cleaning up the moral life of society, dealing with the political and economic mess and setting family life in right order.

Hezekiah saw clearly that the first priority was to deal with the spiritual state of the nation. This meant an act of re-consecration that would both cleanse the people from the sins into which they had been led during Hezekiah's reign, driving out the idolatry and spiritism from among them, and re-dedicate them to the worship and service of God. To do this he wished to remind the nation of their spiritual heritage and in particular of how God had become known to them as a Saviour through the deliverance from Egypt. It was therefore necessary to celebrate Passover as an act of cleansing and of re-consecration. The times were too urgent to wait another eleven months for the traditional time of year for Passover. It was therefore decided to celebrate Passover in the second month.

Tradition is the means by which things of value are conveyed from one generation to the next. In religious matters tradition helps to preserve and to convey the word of God to succeeding generations. But we must never confuse tradition with the word of God. It is the word that is truth, not tradition; tradition is the means of transmission, no more. Hezekiah recognized the difference and refused to allow tradition to hold him back from opening up the nation to the mighty cleansing power of the word of the Lord. He sent out a proclamation to every community of the tribes of Israel both in the north and in the south (2 Chronicles 30:5).

The proclamation Hezekiah issued was well received by all the people. Clearly it was right in the timing of the Lord. The people were aware of the terrible threat from the Assyrians on their northern and eastern borders. They realized that, humanly speaking, their days were numbered. Invasion was inevitable and the Assyrian army appeared to be invincible. They were afraid, and in their fear they were ready to hear and to accept the call from their new young king.

> The hand of God was on the people to give them unity of mind to carry out what the king and his officials had ordered following the word of the Lord. A very large crowd of people assembled in Jerusalem to celebrate the feast of unleavened bread in the second month.
>
> (2 Chronicles 30:12 and 13)

Many of the heads of families had not had time to consecrate themselves and so the Levites killed the Passover lambs 'for all those who were not ceremonially clean and could not consecrate their lambs to the Lord' (2 Chronicles 30:17). Despite the fact that they were not doing everything in the traditional way they were truly seeking God with open hearts and God, who looks upon the heart and not upon the outward appearance, received their worship and restored them into a right relationship with himself: 'The Lord heard Hezekiah and healed the people' (2 Chronicles 30:20).

For seven days they worshipped God and lifted up their offerings to him. They offered not only their sacrifices and their songs of praise; they offered their love and their lives to the Lord. They came before him with a contrite heart for the wickedness into which they had been led, for their lack of faithfulness to God and for the evil and corruption in the nation. They confessed their sinfulness and wept before the Lord asking for his forgiveness and his mercy upon them. Probably they used the words of David when he confessed before the Lord his sin with Bathsheba.

> Have mercy upon me, O God, according to your unfailing love; according to your great compassion blot out my transgressions. Wash away all my iniquity and cleanse

me from my sins . . . Create in me a pure heart, O God, and renew a steadfast spirit within me. Do not cast me from your presence or take your Holy Spirit from me. Restore to me the joy of your salvation and grant me a willing spirit, to sustain me. Then I will teach transgressors your ways, and sinners will turn back to you.

(Psalm 51)

No doubt they discovered the truth that David had also found and expressed in that same psalm – that 'a broken and contrite heart, O God, you will not despise'.

God certainly did not despise the tears of his people who knew that they had been far from him for many years and were longing for his forgiveness, for the joy of being restored into a right relationship with him, and for the embrace of his love.

The whole Temple rang with the praises of the people as they lifted up the name of their God. They praised him with every kind of instrument, they bowed before him, they worshipped and adored him. The very streets of Jerusalem echoed with the praises of the people for the Lord their God, and his glory shone round about.

So powerful was the presence of the Lord among his people that no one wanted to go home. When the Lord is present among his people and the power of his Spirit is being poured out among them, who can bear to depart? Who wants to go back to worldly things, to secular pursuits, to the day-to-day trivia with which we normally fill our lives? They unanimously decided to celebrate for a further seven days – another break with tradition! How the Lord loves to see his people set free from the shackles that bind them and to come in joyful liberty before him, offering themselves unstintingly in worship and service, and giving him their lives without restraint.

Of course the Lord honoured the prayers and praises of his people who had come weeping before him with a contrite heart and now were overflowing with joy as they saw the signs of his gracious acceptance of them and the blessings he brought upon them through the outpouring of his Holy Spirit.

Revival came to the city of Jerusalem!

The entire assembly of Judah rejoiced, along with the priests and Levites and all who had assembled from Israel, including the aliens who had come from Israel and those who lived in Judah. There was great joy in Jerusalem, for since the days of Solomon, son of David king of Israel, there had been nothing like this in Jerusalem.

(2 Chronicles 30:25 and 26)

Even the priests rejoiced! That's what happens in a revival! Even the priests get filled with the Spirit of the Lord and worship him with unrestrained joy! No one cared about traditional propriety. The Lord was present to forgive, to bless and to heal his people.

A notable fact in the record of the events of those remarkable two weeks is that even the aliens who had come to Jerusalem with the Israelites got blessed. These aliens were no doubt some of the new communities planted in Israel by Sennacherib. The Israelites from the North were living in enemy-occupied territory. Some of the aliens among them had probably decided to accompany them to Jerusalem to discover more about the God of the land whom the people were going to worship. They would not, of course, have been allowed into the Temple where only Jews were admitted, but when revival swept through the streets of the city of Jerusalem even the aliens got blessed! Those who were at one time the enemies of Israel were caught up in the praises of God. They saw his glory among the people and they could not refrain from glorifying him themselves and rejoicing in all that he was doing. Even the aliens could not keep back from bowing the knee before the majesty and greatness of God as his presence was revealed among his people.

When revival occurs everyone gets blessed! When the Lord's people come weeping before him all the community around them gets wet. When we seek the Lord with all our heart and mind and spirit, in penitence for our past unfaithfulness and in love and trust, praising him for his loving-kindness, his mercy and his faithfulness, God never fails to respond. As our contrite hearts are renewed, so he pours out his Holy Spirit upon us, bringing spiritual revival and healing to the land. When this happens everyone gets blessed and many more are brought into a saving knowledge of the Lord our God.

I often think of the time when Jesus had gone out in a little fishing boat with the disciples and was lying down asleep in the stern when a fierce storm blew up. It must have been a ferocious storm for the disciples were terrified, and they were fishermen! They earned their living on the Sea of Galilee and knew every fathom of its waters. They were used to sudden storms, and had no doubt sailed their boats through many of them since their boyhood days when they were first taken out by their fathers who were fishermen before them. But this storm was different. They were quite sure the tiny boat would capsize as it was being tossed like a cork on the enormous waves and battered by hurricane-force winds. It seems incredible that amid all this noise and turmoil Jesus could still be peacefully sleeping in the back of the boat! The disciples eventually woke him up and begged his help as they were convinced they would soon be drowning.

With a word of command Jesus exercised authority over wind and wave. Immediately there was calm. The wind disappeared and the waves subsided. A great calm descended even more rapidly than the storm had blown up. It was eerie! The disciples knelt before Jesus in awe. Who was this that even the wind and the waves obeyed? Surely it could be none other than God himself incarnate in the person of the Messiah.

I like to exercise my imagination at this point, although I do not think this is a flight of fantasy. I believe that on the Sea of Galilee there were many other little boats at the time of that storm. When Jesus stood up in response to the request of his own disciples and stilled the storm all the other boats got blessed! Many other fishermen who were afraid for their lives rejoiced in the sudden calm. What an opportunity was presented to Peter and the others later in the day to witness for the Lord! Everyone would be talking about the fierce storm and the sudden calm, down at the Fisherman's Arms and on the beach where they were mending their nets. 'Yes,' said Peter, 'and I can tell you why the great calm happened. It was Jesus, our Master, God's Messiah; he just stretched out his hand, said the word of command, and the calm followed. Surely this man is God's own Messiah and you should accept him as we have!'

When God acts to bless his people in response to their prayers and their cries for help, all the community around them gets blessed. That's what happens in a revival. That's what happened in Jerusalem during Hezekiah's revival. Even the aliens got blessed!

The revival had an immediate effect throughout the nation. There were many things wrong in the national life which were clearly revealed to the people and they set about changing the whole order of society. The first thing they did was to smash down the altars of Baal and root out idolatry in every town and village throughout the land. They 'smashed the sacred stones and cut down the Asherah poles. They destroyed the high places and the altars throughout Judah and Benjamin and in Ephraim and Manasseh' (2 Chronicles 31:1). When they had finished cleaning out the witchcraft and the idolatry they then began the task of re-ordering the right worship of God. Priests and Levites were assigned to divisions and each of them given their tasks, their times to be on-duty and their times to be off-duty, as well as the times that they would actually be officiating at worship. They even appointed groups to sing the praise of the Lord at the gates of the Temple so that all the passers-by would be continually reminded of his presence among them (2 Chronicles 31:2).

Clearly Hezekiah was intent on getting the nation into a right spiritual order, a right relationship with God so that they would be strong in the Lord – well-armed by the power of the Holy Spirit. Hezekiah knew what was coming. He knew that the forces arrayed against them were too much for them, but God had given this young man great spiritual insight so that he understood the nature of the battle. It was not simply physical warfare but spiritual warfare for which he had to prepare the people. He re-introduced tithing and sound teaching of the people.

Then, 'after all that Hezekiah had so faithfully done, Sennacherib king of Assyria came and invaded Judah' (2 Chronicles 32:1). In that terse sentence in the recorded history of this period there lies the reason for all the tremendous spiritual activity that had been taking place in the life of the nation.

God's timely outpouring of his Holy Spirit, which brought spiritual revival upon the nation, was for the purpose of preparing them for the coming battle, giving their leaders a spirit of discernment to enable them to understand the true nature of the battle, and building the nation up spiritually so that they would be able to trust the Lord and be absolutely obedient to him when the storm clouds of violence broke upon them. His purpose in giving revival was to build up the spiritual life of the nation to enable them to resist the enemy and to reach out to the Lord their God with such complete trust that he would be able to work through them and accomplish a mighty miracle through the faith, the expectation, the intercessions and the believing prayers of his people. This provides us with a model of God's purposes and his ways with his people.

As soon as Sennacherib crossed the borders of Judah and began to lay siege to some of the outlying provincial cities Hezekiah set about the task of preparing Jerusalem to resist the enemy. They had already been laying in store extra consignments of food and provisions in the Temple store-rooms. Now he tackled the water supply, even blocking off springs and streams that could be of use to the enemy. He repaired breaches in the city's defences and built an outer wall, with reinforced terraces on the main walls, to give a first line of defence.

Hezekiah prepared the people for the coming battle to

defend the city and ensured that everyone knew exactly his right place and what he should do in the face of the enemy. But Hezekiah knew that the real nature of the battle was spiritual and not physical. It would not be won on the field of military conflict. It would be won only through the power and authority of Almighty God. He saw that the key to success in the coming battle was not simply that the whole nation should be rightly ordered and disciplined, with every family and individual in a right relationship with each other and with their God, although this was an essential pre-requisite.

Hezekiah saw that this was a battle that could only be won by God. Only he had the power to overcome such an enemy, but Hezekiah had the spiritual wisdom to know the ways of God. He knew that God works through the faith, through the believing prayers and the trust of his people. This was why the nation had to be in right order before the Lord and why all the social and physical preparations of the nation were necessary. But having done all, Hezekiah knew their human limitations. He knew that it was only the Lord who could give them the victory and he knew the right moment to turn in absolute trust to the Lord, saying in effect: 'Father, we have done all that is humanly possible for us to do. The enemy has come against us and we are powerless to resist him. Our eyes are turned to you, Lord, for in you is the power and the victory. We put our trust completely in you and ask you to cover us with your protection and save us, O Lord our God and our Redeemer.' God always honours such faith among his people and he honoured the faithful inter-cessions of Hezekiah.

It was during these days of busy preparation that Hezekiah fell sick. No doubt the responsibility, the anxiety and the heavy work load took their toll of his physical strength. Hezekiah was fortunate to have at his side in Jerusalem, Isaiah, one of the greatest prophets who ever lived. It may be that Isaiah had a share in teaching the young Hezekiah to know the Lord before he came to the throne. Certainly the King was used to turning to the great man of God to pray things through together and to seek guidance. It was to him he now turned in his illness and Isaiah confirmed that he was going to die.

Hezekiah could not believe that the Lord would remove him from leadership in the nation with his task undone, the people still facing the onslaught of the relentless enemy. He saw his illness as a test of his faith and committed it to the Lord, weeping bitterly and praying for healing. Isaiah returned with new instructions from the Lord: 'Go and tell Hezekiah, this is what the Lord, the God of your father David, says, I have heard your prayer and seen your tears; I will add fifteen years to your life. And I will deliver you and this city from the hand of the king of Assyria, I will defend this city' (Isaiah 38:4-6).

Hezekiah was indeed healed, which must have strengthened his faith immeasurably and added a fresh dimension of personal witness to his leadership. He continued to prepare the people with renewed zeal and confidence.

He appointed military officers over the people and assembled them before him in the square at the city gate and encouraged them with these words: 'Be strong and courageous, do not be afraid or discouraged because of the king of Assyria and the vast army with him, for there is a greater power with us than with him. With him is only the arm of flesh, but with us is the Lord our God to help us fight our battles.' And the people gained confidence from what Hezekiah the king of Judah said.

(2 Chronicles 32:6-8)

When a threatening letter arrived from the commander of Sennacherib's army, demanding the surrender of Jerusalem, Hezekiah knew what to do. The letter was insulting to God. It declared that none of the gods of the other nations had been able to withstand the armies of Assyria and neither would the God of Judah, he had no more power to resist Sennacherib than the gods of any of the other nations. Hezekiah 'went up

:o the Temple of the Lord and spread it out before the Lord.
And Hezekiah prayed to the Lord' (Isaiah 37:14 and 15).

The answer came swiftly, first in a prophecy through
Isaiah and secondly through the direct action of the Lord.

> This is what the Lord says concerning the king of Assyria;
> he will not enter this city or shoot an arrow here. He will
> not come before it with shield or build a siege ramp against
> it. By the way that he came he will return; he will not enter
> the city, declares the Lord. I will defend this city and save
> it for my sake and for the sake of my servant David!
>
> (vv. 33–35)

The next thing we read is of a plague sweeping through the
Assyrian army, decimating its ranks and causing
Sennacherib to withdraw in haste. The tattered remnant of
his once proud and victorious army made its way in
disorderly retreat across the hundreds of miles from Judah
to Nineveh. Sennacherib never recovered from the disgrace
of his defeat. He had once been the commander of the most
powerful army the world had ever known but the forces
against him were too great. The chronicler records that 'King
Hezekiah and the prophet Isaiah son of Amoz cried out in
prayer to heaven about this' (2 Chronicles 32:20). What a
powerful combination! Hezekiah and Isaiah standing
together in prayer. King and prophet, both mighty men of
God standing together and calling upon the Lord in absolute
trust and confidence. There is no force on earth, human or
demonic, that could stand against the power released by such
prayer!

> Then the angel of the Lord went out and put to death a
> hundred and eighty-five thousand men in the Assyrian
> camp. When the people got up the next morning – there
> were all the dead bodies! So Sennacherib king of Assyria
> broke camp and withdrew. He returned to Nineveh and
> stayed there. One day, while he was worshipping in the
> temple of his God Nisroch, his sons Adrammelech and
> Sharezer cut him down with the sword.   (Isaiah 37:36–38)

Christians in all the nations throughout the world need to hear the message of Hezekiah's revival. It is not simply a message to build up our faith and courage as we read of the confidence of a great man of God. It contains a vital message that God wants to convey to all his people everywhere. It is a message concerning the nature of the battle that is facing us. The forces arrayed against mankind that are threatening the very survival of our civilization and the lives of millions of men and women and children in many nations are not simply human forces. This is spiritual warfare! The nations of the world are being driven by the forces of evil, the enemy of mankind who wishes to see us destroyed. It is the enemy's purpose to return the world to the primitive chaos and void out of which God created order at the beginning of time (Genesis 1:2).

There is massive evidence today that the nations are set on the path that leads to destruction. This evidence is all around us in the secular world; it is clearly written in the word of God in scripture and it is being conveyed by prophetic revelation to the people of God who have ears to hear and a heart open to God. The forces at work in our world are so powerful that humanly speaking they are unstoppable. They will carry mankind to the edge of the precipice and over into the abyss of death. We are not simply up against the arm of flesh but against the principalities and powers, 'against the powers of this dark world and against the spiritual forces of evil in the heavenly realms' (Ephesians 6:12).

It is essential that the people of God recognize the true nature of the battle in order that they may rightly be able to speak and act within their own nations, and that they may be open to what God is saying to them as the storm clouds gather across the world and the closing days of this age come upon us.

The message God is urgently conveying to his people is the same as that which he gave to Jehoshaphat in another day when his people were under the threat of annihilation: 'The battle is not yours but God's' (2 Chronicles 20:15). God is telling us that only he can defeat the forces of evil that are threatening to sweep the nations into chaos and destruction. He is longing to use this occasion for a mighty act of salvation that will witness to the whole of mankind. To do this he needs the absolute faith and confidence and trust of his people. He needs us to turn to him as the people did in the time of Jehoshaphat and to say as they did, 'for we have no power to face this vast army that is attacking us. We do not know what to do, but our eyes are upon you' (2 Chronicles 20:12). That is the kind of faith which God is looking for in his people.

It is for this reason that God is giving a fresh outpouring of the Holy Spirit in our own generation. The Church world-wide is today growing at a faster rate than it has ever done since the Holy Spirit was first poured out upon the followers of Jesus. On every continent the Church is growing, and in most nations too. Many of the newer nations, in what we know as the Third World, are experiencing a spiritual awakening of immense proportions. We will speak of this further in chapter eight. There is overwhelming evidence that God is at work among his people. He is calling us back to faith in him and using the present emergency – the threat to world peace that is becoming more and more apparent to people throughout the world – to call us back to a fresh commitment to him.

God is longing to give revival or spiritual awakening in every land so that he can arm his people for battle and, in his own perfect timing, call upon them to speak his word and witness to the nations. He is preparing a mighty act of salvation that will witness to those who do not know him that the whole world may see his glory and know his power and majesty and glorify his Son that in the name of Jesus every knee shall bow, and every tongue confess him King of glory now.

He can only carry out his great purposes for mankind through the faith and obedience of his people; that is the way he has willed it. He has created man in his own image and called us into obedience to him, given us knowledge of his fatherly love and made it possible for us to enter into a right relationship with himself through the blood of the New Covenant established through the Cross of Jesus Christ. But his good purposes can be thwarted. His best will for mankind is being opposed not simply by the onslaught of the enemy but by the faithlessness and unresponsiveness of his own people.

It is for this reason that God is urgently calling upon us today and giving a fresh outpouring of his Holy Spirit. He has a special task for his people and he is urgently directing us towards it. We shall look at this task in the next chapter.

CHAPTER SEVEN

Gideon's Army

In a time of great danger or national stress in ancient Israel God always raised up men or women whom he endued with special gifts and to whom he entrusted special tasks. This did not mean that God had no use for the rest of the nation, or that he rejected the bulk of his people and simply chose a favoured few. Indeed God never rejects us; it is we who reject him and refuse to hear the things he is saying to us or to respond when he calls. It does mean that God knows the task that is needed to be undertaken in any period of time and he knows the gifts that he has given to each person. He also knows our likely response, or unresponsiveness. Where there are special tasks to be undertaken he directs a particular appeal to the person who has that special combination of gifts that are required for the moment.

Such a man for such a time was Gideon. He was strong, muscular, courageous. He was a man of wisdom, discernment and sound judgement – all the qualities needed for leadership. Above all Gideon was a man of great faith in God. Yet when we first meet this 'mighty man of valour' we find him cowering in a winepress at his father's farm for fear of the marauding bands of Arab tribesmen who were plaguing the land and pilfering the produce from Israelite settlements. He had actually gone into hiding for fear of the Midianites while beating out some wheat. He didn't dare thresh his wheat out on the threshing-floor – the natural place, where the wind would blow away the chaff – he preferred to suffer the dust and discomfort of crouching in a cramped winepress than face up to the enemy all Israel feared.

We are told that for seven years these Midianite and

Amalekite tribesmen had swept across the land like a plague of locusts, stealing the sheep, oxen and asses. They came in huge numbers, the tents of their camps stretched across the countryside so that 'it was impossible to count the men and their camels' (Judges 6:5).

Gideon received a divine visitation. God timed it perfectly, catching him skulking in the winepress and addressing him as a 'mighty warrior'. This is surely strong evidence for God's good sense of humour! This shouldn't really surprise us; if we can laugh at things, surely God can too; after all, he made us in his own image.

Gideon, caught in a compromising position that certainly made him feel rather foolish, to say the least, didn't really see the funny side of it when he was told to go and use the mighty strength he had got to save Israel and drive the Midianites out of the land. He protested strongly.

'But Lord,' Gideon asked, 'how can I save Israel, my clan is the weakest in Manasseh, and I am the least in my family.' The Lord answered, 'I will be with you and you will strike down the Midianites as if they were but one man.' (Judges 6:15 and 16)

After this when Gideon is assured that God really has spoken to him he begins to respond, although very timidly. He knows that the first priority is to clean up the spiritual life of the nation and the right place to start is in his own community. So he begins by hacking down the Asherah pole and destroying the altar to Baal in his own village. He was afraid of the reaction it would provoke even within his own family, but he was even more afraid of disobedience to the Lord now that he was sure of his word of command. As a compromise, he obeyed, but he did it by night!

Of course you couldn't keep an event like that secret in a small community, and soon everyone knew that it was Gideon who had thrown down the altar of Baal. Amid the ensuing uproar Gideon's father had the good sense to prevent mob violence against his son by declaring that it was Baal's altar that had been destroyed and if he was a god he should prove it by striking Gideon down! This somehow made sense even to those who had been spiritually confused by years of idolatry, and when nothing happened to Gideon his prestige and his confidence rose.

Soon after this an enormous force of Arabs from many different tribes crossed over the river Jordan and camped in the valley of Jezreel. Their clear intention was to swarm across the land in even greater numbers than they had ever done before, destroying everything in their path and wreaking havoc in the Israelite communities. It was then that a radical change took place in Gideon's life. The Spirit of the Lord came upon him and totally transformed him. The old fearfulness and hesitation left him and the strong determined leader emerged, the man of God with absolute faith and trust in the Lord. He blew the trumpet, summoning the men of his own community to follow him. They obeyed instantly. He sent messengers throughout the neighbouring tribes of Israel calling the nation to prepare for war under his leadership. Thirty-two thousand men from all over Israel responded to the call to arms and readily gathered to a man whom they recognized as inspired by the Lord.

Clear evidence of Gideon's inspired leadership is seen in that he didn't rush straight into battle as soon as he saw the mighty response to his call. Instead he waited upon the Lord in prayer and received his instructions from God.

> You have too many men for me to deliver Midian into their hands. In order that Israel may not boast against me that her own strength has saved her, announce now to the people, 'Anyone who trembles with fear may turn back and leave Mount Gilead.'   (Judges 7:2 and 3)

Twenty-two thousand men left, leaving just ten thousand. It wasn't simply that God wanted to ensure that he was given all the glory for the coming victory, but years of idolatry had sapped the spiritual life of Israel and they had to be taught the lesson that everything had gone wrong in the life of the nation because of their disobedience. Things could not be put right by taking matters into their own hands and walking in their own strength. It was only the Lord who could deliver them, and this had to be made abundantly plain to them. If their army was reasonably large, even if they were still outnumbered by three or four to one, they could say that the victory was won by their own feat of arms. God had to ensure that the number involved in routing the enemy was so ridiculously small that the victory had come not by might, nor by power, but by his Spirit! So the command came again, 'There are still too many men'.

Now at this point we come to the real heart of the message. I believe that God is raising a 'Gideon's army' now for the special task that he is committing into the hands of those whom he is calling up for service in these critical days. God is calling together a kind of 'Special Service Unit' that consists of those who are filled with his Spirit, men and women from every nation who are responsive to his call, and to whom he has given particular gifts that he wishes to use for the special task to which they are called. Before we look at that task we need to study carefully the characteristics of that small band of men that Gideon led into battle and through whom God routed the enemy. By such a study we will gain a clearer understanding of what the Lord is doing among his people today. There are seven characteristics that we need to note.

Seven Characteristics of Gideon's Army

1. COURAGE

The first characteristic of the men who went with Gideon was that they were not afraid to face the enemy. This does not mean that they had no fear. The man who experiences no fear in the face of danger either has no imagination or is just plain stupid! Such a man would have no place in Gideon's army, as he could endanger the whole operation by his lack of perception of danger and this could lead him into reckless action. The kind of courage God was looking for in the men who served in Gideon's special service unit was a keen awareness of the dangers confronting them yet a relentless determination to face the enemy despite the human odds against them. That is real courage – a recognition of the danger, but a determination to face the enemy and go through with the action.

Thirty-two thousand men came forward in Israel in response to Gideon's call to fight the Midianites. Most of them came forward with fear and trembling because they knew both the size and the ruthlessness of the enemy they would be facing. Gideon received instructions from God to announce 'Anyone who trembles with fear may turn back and leave Mount Gilead', whereupon two-thirds of the fighting men whose knees were knocking and teeth chattering with fear turned away from the battle front. The ten thousand who remained were brave enough to persevere despite their fears. This was the kind of courage that was needed in Gideon's army. The ten thousand were men who showed perseverance when the odds against them made the task appear hopeless. They continued to face the enemy despite their fears and were determined to go through with the action whatever the cost to themselves. That kind of faithful perseverance is part of the fruit of the Spirit that Paul refers to in Galatians 5:22.

2. DISCERNMENT

Courage alone was not a sufficient qualification for membership of Gideon's army. His special service unit had to have other qualities that would lift them above the average courageous man going into battle to slog it out with the enemy. This was a special kind of battle and it required a special kind of strategy. Therefore it required men with a special gift of discernment. They had to be men who were alert to every move of the enemy, ready and prepared to adjust their own actions according to their interpretation of the signs around them. It was essential therefore that they should be able to interpret those signs. They had to be watchful, wide awake and not miss anything that was happening. We would say, 'they had to have eyes in the back of their heads'. Certainly their eyes and ears and minds had to see, hear and rightly interpret all that was going on around them.

God told Gideon that the ten thousand were still too many.

> Take them down to the water, and I will sift them out for you there. If I say, 'This one shall go with you', he shall go; but if I say, 'This one shall not go with you', he shall not go. (Judges 7:4)

Gideon gave the order for the men to go down to a nearby stream, no doubt a few at a time so that he could watch them closely. How the men must have longed for their turn to fall out of that military parade after the many hours of marshalling under the hot sun, whilst Gideon assembled the army and checked the whole original thirty-two thousand men with their divisional officers and company commanders. It was a long time to stand in the heat and many of the remaining ten thousand probably wished they had taken the easy option and gone with the twenty-two thousand who had returned to their tents. How each company must have run down that slope to the bank of the stream when the order was given and it was their turn to go. The eagerness with which they longed to quench their thirst and wet their parched lips and dry throats was reflected in their behaviour when they reached the water's edge. The great majority of the ten thousand flung themselves to the ground, plunged their heads into the stream and sucked in the cool water greedily.

There were just three hundred men who exercised the kind of self-control which is also mentioned by Paul as part of the fruit of the Spirit. They did not allow the desires of the flesh to blind them to the fact that they were in enemy-occupied territory! They did not allow the desires of the flesh to plunge them into danger. They knew the enemy was all around them. They knew they had to remain watchful for his presence. They knew they should never relax their guard but be always alert to the enemy's movements. While the majority of the ten thousand were giving way to the demands of the flesh just three hundred men refrained from flinging themselves down on to the ground and sucking in the water that their bodies craved. Instead, they knelt, scooped the water up in their hands to their mouths and lapped, so that their eyes could continue to take in the scene around them and their ears could ever be alert for a sound of the enemy.

It was this quality of watchfulness and self-control that distinguished the three hundred from the ten thousand men of courage who had volunteered to go with Gideon to take on the might of Midian. The three hundred had a spirit of discernment which enabled them to be aware of the danger around them and not to be blinded by personal desire.

3. FAITH

The Lord said to Gideon, 'With the three hundred men who lapped I will save you and give the Midianites into your hands.' (Judges 7:7)

Gideon had already separated out the three hundred men who lapped with their hands to their mouths. When he conveyed to them that they were the ones whom God had chosen to use for a mighty victory over Midian, even the most courageous among them would have faltered if he had not been a man of great faith. It was their faith in God and their utter trust in his word that enabled them to accept the assignment they were given. This is where faith can be clearly distinguished from mere human trust. The three hundred gladly and willingly accepted the task given to them not because they trusted in Gideon's leadership, although clearly they did trust him, but because they had faith in God.

Trust in human leadership is based upon a logical deduction, or at least upon a calculus of probabilities. On the basis of a man's past record we reckon him to be worthy of trust and therefore we will follow his leadership because we trust his judgement. But Gideon had no illustrious record of past achievement in the field of military leadership. He was a farmer's son with no previous experience and no military training! He had been suddenly catapulted into the exalted position of General in command of the national army solely on the basis of his relationship with God. So far as we know Gideon's only achievement was that he had broken down the altar of a local god and survived the wrath of his village community. Undoubtedly word of this had gone around widely as evidence of his absolute loyalty to God, but it was because men believed that he had been appointed by God to the leadership of the army of the Lord that Gideon was trusted.

What we are emphasizing is that in the view of the people the army of Israel was the Lord's army and whoever was appointed by him to lead the army did so in the power and under the authority of the Lord. Thus the commander of the army was not simply a man acting as a military strategist. He was a divinely appointed leader carrying out what was, at least in part, a prophetic task. It was his responsibility to listen to God and to interpret his word to those who placed themselves under his command. From the standpoint of the ordinary soldiers in the army, they had not chosen the commander, neither had he been elected by some kind of national referendum. He had been appointed by God. There were clear signs of the anointing of the Spirit of God upon his life. Therefore in trusting him they were exercising faith in God.

When Gideon told the three hundred that God intended to save the nation from the Midianites through them they accepted the task as a divine calling. They had absolute confidence in God's ability to carry out his word. If he said he would do something, he would do it. If he gave them a task, he would supply the strength. Their trust was not in the ability of men but in the power of God.

Thus the three hundred went into battle with Gideon their leader, the man of God, united in spirit and bound together by that quietness and confidence in God that is the characteristic of faith. They had the faith, the absolute confidence in God, that removes mountains. When God told them to go forward, they knew that there was no power on earth that could stop them! That is faith!

4. OBEDIENCE

It was this faith in God that gave them the confidence to be obedient. When God said, 'Let all the other men go, each to his own place' (Judges 7:7), they obeyed. 'So Gideon sent the rest of the Israelites to their tents but kept the three hundred, who took over the provisions and trumpets of the others' (v. 8).

It is interesting to note that the ten thousand volunteers were not sent home. They were sent back to their tents, back to base camp. They would be needed soon, but it was the men of the special unit who were to form Gideon's army and through whom God would bring about a mighty miracle that would cause the rout of the enemy.

The three hundred must have been mystified by the swiftly moving events. They had come to Mount Gilead in response to Gideon's call, which they believed to be a call from God, as part of an army of thirty-two thousand men. They had seen that multitude of men axed to a third, and now nine thousand seven hundred of the remnant were being stood down. What was even more puzzling was that instead of being given extra swords and conventional weaponry, they were given trumpets and household utensils!

To men lacking in faith the whole operation would have looked ludicrous. But to men with the eyes of faith it was all part of God's preparation for accomplishing the miracle he planned. He was selecting ordinary men such as they were and ordinary everyday material commodities to carry out his mighty purposes.

These were the ways of God. This was exactly what Jesus did. He took a group of fishermen and other nobodies to be his closest followers, and he took ordinary material things like bread and wine to give to them as his body.

The three hundred did not understand the strategy God was pursuing, but they had the faith to be obedient. If God said to take trumpets and earthenware jars and waxen torches, then those were the things they would take. It was simple obedience based upon absolute confidence in God. That confidence and trust in his word came from faith.

God was teaching, not only the three hundred of Gideon's army, but the whole nation of Israel an important spiritual lesson. When God takes over the warfare it is no longer conventional warfare, fought with conventional weapons and human strategy. It is spiritual warfare fought with the weapons that he chooses and under the strategy that he directs. For such a battle God requires people who will give him absolute obedience. God could not have given them the victory if the three hundred had questioned the orders he gave or had sat down and debated the strategy that he was apparently following. They simply accepted that when God stepped into the human arena to take over the direction of the battle they would not be able to understand his ways, but that that didn't matter. He was in control. He saw the end from the beginning. They knew the outcome was assured, the victory would be won. What was required of them was to trust and obey! When God gave the orders, however ridiculous they seemed to human ears and eyes, they obeyed.

The three hundred were men of obedience. When God gave the orders, they didn't question them.

5. VISION

Now the camp of Midian lay below him in the valley. During that night the Lord said to Gideon, 'Get up, go down against the camp, because I am going to give it into your hands. If you are afraid to attack, go down to the camp with your servant Purah and listen to what they are saying. Afterwards, you will be encouraged to attack the camp.'   (Judges 7:8–11)

Of course Gideon was afraid to attack the camp. He knew perfectly well that he was going up against a powerful, well-armed enemy. Although he had the confidence of faith in God and the assurance that he would give them victory, as yet Gideon lacked vision. God had not yet revealed to him his whole counsel on the coming battle. Gideon had simply been acting in obedience one step at a time, confident that in his own perfect timing God would reveal to him his overall plan.

As a man of God, Gideon knew that God could speak to him in many different ways. He could bring a picture into his mind whilst he was awake or asleep, he could speak to him directly by bringing words clearly into his mind, he could use a scene from the natural environment surrounding him, or an incident that happened close by to speak into the situation. Gideon was fully aware that God does not limit himself to one means of communication but has many ways of speaking to his servants who have ears to hear and eyes to see and a mind open to God.

Gideon knew that he was not yet ready to go into battle until he had been given that clear vision that only God could communicate to him. Vision is linked with the spiritual gift of wisdom in the New Testament of which Paul speaks in 1 Corinthians 12:8. When a man is anointed by the Holy Spirit for a special task, as was Gideon, by that same Spirit he is given spiritual insight – a wisdom that carries him beyond his human understanding. The spirit of wisdom enables him to perceive the nature of the conflict and the strategy God is using to accomplish the victory. Over and above such an understanding of the path and direction in which God is leading, the Holy Spirit reveals that part of the divine plan, or the overall purposes of God, that is necessary for the anointed leader to know in order to carry out his task. That is vision.

Vision reveals the overall purposes of God. It enables a man to stand in the council of the Almighty and to hear and see things that transcend the temporal, that go beyond the limits of finite human reason and understanding (Jer. 23:22).

Gideon was used to standing in the council of God, so when the Lord told him to go down to the camp of Midian where he would speak to him, despite all the obvious dangers, Gideon obeyed. He and his servant crept down to the outposts of the camp where the camels of the Arab tribesmen were as numerous as 'the sand on the sea shore' (v. 12).

> Gideon arrived just as a man was telling a friend his dream. 'I had a dream,' he was saying. 'A round loaf of barley bread came tumbling into the Midianite camp. It struck the tent with such force that the tent overturned and collapsed.' His friend responded, 'This can be nothing other than the sword of Gideon son of Joash, the Israelite. God has given the Midianites and the whole camp into his hand.' (Judges 7:13 and 14)

Gideon instantly recognized the significance of both the dream and the interpretation. Even the special significance of the little round loaf of barley bread was not lost on him. Barley was the lightest form of bread. A barley loaf was not heavy and filling and fully satisfying like regular wheat bread. In fact, a little barley loaf was despised by people with healthy appetites. They wanted full wheat bread and nothing less. A barley loaf was so light it was insignificant and could never satisfy a hungry man.

Gideon saw that it was with just such a despised and insignificant instrument that God intended to bring about a mighty miracle of deliverance in Israel. Probably, through the ministry of the Holy Spirit, Gideon already knew the teaching that Paul was to make explicit more than a thousand years later.

> For though we live in the world, we do not wage war as the world does. The weapons we fight with are not the weapons of the world. On the contrary, they have divine power to demolish strongholds.
>
> (2 Corinthians 10:3 and 4)

As he heard the dream and its interpretation the vision came. Gideon stood in the council of the Almighty. He saw the significance of each instruction he had so far been given. He perceived the overall purposes of God in giving deliverance to Israel. He was given the insight to understand the strategy of the Lord. His task now was to convey the vision to the special service unit who had been called by the Lord to serve with him. Once they had the vision they only had to await the timing of the Lord to go in the power of his Spirit and the strength of his might.

6. TRAINING

As soon as the vision had been communicated to Gideon and he perceived the strategy he was to follow he immediately set about training the three hundred. He left the enemy camp and returned to his own men full of the power of the Holy Spirit, worshipping and praising God. When vision comes and a man knows he has stood in the council of the Lord his own spirit leaps within him in response to the presence of the Holy Spirit. He is filled with awe and wonder that he who is Almighty, Creator of the ends of the universe, should speak to him who is so creaturely, a mere human being.

When Gideon came back to his men in the power of the Spirit, his voice no doubt carried a new authority. He began training them for the task that lay ahead and telling them of the good plans that God had revealed to him whereby he would bring about an amazing victory over the enemy. Through this victory God would also teach his people such a spiritual lesson that would bring them into a fresh understanding of his ways and into a new obedience through a restored and right relationship with himself.

> He returned to the camp of Israel and called out, 'Get up! the Lord has given the Midianite camp into your hands.' Dividing the three hundred men into three companies, he placed trumpets and empty jars into the hands of all of them, with torches inside. 'Watch me,' he told them. 'Follow my lead.' (Judges 7:15-17)

Gideon's major concern was that each man should clearly understand the overall strategy. Moreover, each man needed to know his own task within that strategy. They were to move in three companies so that the enemy would be surrounded on all sides. In order to accomplish this encircling movement every man had an essential part to play. If one was missing the circle would not be complete. Each man had to see the importance of the job he was doing and each one had to know exactly where he should be at the appointed time when the action began. This required training.

Gideon set about the task of carefully preparing his men for the coming battle with all the zeal and energy of a General commanding his troops, while at the same time he was conscious that the weapons they would be using were not the weapons of conventional warfare. This was a different kind of battle and so too would be the manner of the victory.

Gideon had to carry out some careful training of the three companies in order that each man should be able to handle the strange weapons that were put into his hands. It was not an easy assignment to carry a trumpet in one hand and to hold in the other an empty earthenware jar with a lighted torch inside. The three companies had to be familiar with the route they were to take down the hillside, to know the point at which each would stand around the edge of the enemy camp and to understand exactly what to do and when to do it.

Gideon told them that when he gave the signal each man was to blow his trumpet, then they were to smash the jars and grasp the torches in their left hands while holding the trumpets in their right hands. Then they were to shout 'A sword for the Lord and for Gideon!' They were then to continue blowing their trumpets and shouting 'For the Lord and for Gideon', while holding the torches aloft in their left hands and giving further blasts on the trumpets. Gideon told them that it was essential they should maintain their positions, doing exactly as instructed and not moving from where they stood until they saw the victory of the Lord.

The object of the training was that each man should be properly prepared. Gideon's army knew the strategy of the Lord, for through the eyes of Gideon they had seen the vision he had revealed. They knew the part they were to play. They were prepared for the coming battle. They were men who went out in the confidence of the Lord to do the task for which they had been prepared. That is the value of training.

7. DISCIPLINE

Even the most careful training and preparation would have been thwarted if Gideon's army had not been a band of disciplined men. All their faith and spiritual insight and training would have come to naught if there had not been absolute self-control in Gideon's army. Once they left their own camp and began the descent towards the enemy stronghold each man was on his own, yet each was inextricably bound to the other. If one failed, they all failed. If one man lost self-control and broke the strict code of discipline, the whole operation foundered.

If one man in the special service unit had broken the absolute silence with a whispered word, or if one man had stumbled and sent a loose stone crashing down the hillside, or if a man had dropped his jar or even sneezed during that silent descent to take up their allotted positions around the enemy camp, the guards would have been alerted, the tiny band would have been discovered, the enemy would have been roused and Gideon's army would have been slaughtered without a sword to defend them. They were an utterly disciplined group. Each man knew the responsibility he carried for the team, for the task, for the nation and for the Lord!

Even when they reached the outskirts of the enemy camp if one man had anticipated the order to shout or if one man had shown the light of his torch too soon before everyone had taken up their positions, the whole operation would have been endangered. Discipline and self-control were essential.

When the three companies had taken up their positions around the edge of the enemy camp, at the right moment, just as the middle watch of the night had come on duty, Gideon blew the trumpet. Instantly three hundred trumpets blasted the night air and startled the wits out of the confused minds of the sleepy Midianites, Amalekites and other Eastern tribesmen who had invaded the land. In the next instant the jars were smashed, sending a terrifying sound through the camp. Then the lighted torches were held aloft by three hundred men with powerful lungs bellowing 'For the Lord and for Gideon'. Then the trumpets sounded again and again, again and again. The men were acting as one man. They were in absolute harmony, complete unity. They were an utterly disciplined band of men.

The terrifying suddenness of the night onslaught upon their ears startled the enemy out of their minds. They no longer behaved like a trained fighting force or even like rational human beings. The sight of their entire camp ringed with men holding aloft flaming torches in one hand and with the other hand holding those blaring trumpets was enough to instil panic into even the bravest among them. After all, if this was the size of the trumpet band what was the size of the army they led! What mighty multitude of swordsmen would accompany such a powerful band of trumpeters!

Panic spread through the enemy ranks within seconds. As each man rushed out of his tent, every shadow in the night thrown by those lighted torches was a threat. Each man lunged at his neighbour with drawn sword. Inside that ring of light from the flaming torches, and spurred on by the terrifying blasts of the trumpets, the enemy fell upon each other. In the camp of Midian terror reigned! It was a night of panic and slaughter.

Throughout the mêlée of confusion, danger and death, Gideon's army maintained their positions. Not a man moved from his place. Not one lowered his flaming torch or ceased to blow his trumpet until the order was given. The enemy was routed! The remnants of Midian began to flee across the countryside! The three hundred, with the unconventional weapons and the mighty faith in their God, were an utterly disciplined army.

The Outcome of the Battle

Once the tattered remnants of the enemy army were on the run the main task of Gideon's army was completed. It was at this stage that he called out the whole army of Israel. God had already routed the enemy through the special service unit; now it was time for every able-bodied man in the nation to come out, drive the enemy from the borders of the land and share in the spoils and the joy of victory. No doubt the ten thousand volunteers who were in the camp up on the hill were the first to come into action, but Gideon also 'sent messengers throughout the hill country of Ephraim, saying, "Come down against the Midianites and seize the waters of the Jordan ahead of them as far as Beth Barah"' (Judges 7:24).

Israel learned the lesson that God calls certain individuals to undertake specific tasks according to the demands of the times in which they live but that all his people are needed, none is redundant, all are called into his service. The three hundred men of Gideon's army who were used to begin the rout of the enemy were not disbanded as soon as the enemy began to flee. They were part of the wider army of the Lord. They did not act as though they were some élite body who were thereby exempt from the strenuous and much less glamorous task of chasing the enemy across the countryside and clearing him out of the land.

Gideon's three hundred took their share in the general job that had to be done alongside the rest of the people, despite the fact that they were already very tired from the demands of their training and from the taut nerves of their incredible night's exploits. We read of them keeping up the chase despite their tiredness.

> Gideon and his three hundred men, exhausted yet keeping up the pursuit, came to the Jordan and crossed it.
>
> (Judges 8:4)

God was teaching his people that he has no favourites. God only has one people, one family. Each person is equally loved and valued by him. From time to time, according to the demands of the age, he calls certain individuals and lays upon them specific responsibilities, tasks to be undertaken in his service and for which he supplies the gifts.

When God calls any individual into his service for a specific task he supplies the enabling. In this way God prevents his children from going in their own strength to undertake tasks that only he can do. He uses those who are especially sensitive to his purposes and responsive to his will, who understand the nature of the battle and the odds against them achieving anything in their own strength. Thus when the victory comes they give all the glory to him. His praises fill the mouths of his people and he is able to draw them closer to him in love, in worship and adoration.

The Message for Today

In the closing years of the twentieth century, with the world plunging into economic confusion, political chaos and international conflict on a vast and unimaginable scale, God is calling together a Gideon's army. It is a special service unit endued with spiritual gifts to enable them to undertake the specific tasks to which God is calling them. They are not from any one nation but from all the nations. They are not an army of volunteers but an army called and chosen by God. Like Gideon's army, they are chosen from among the volunteers who respond to God's call to action.

This, however, does not mean that God has rejected all the rest of the volunteers, those who are open to him and responsive to his will. Neither does it mean that the special service unit are in any way a favoured élite. If they began to exalt themselves above their brethren they would immediately be rejected by the Lord. Spiritual élitism is not tolerated in the kingdom! He who exalts himself will be humbled, those are the words of Jesus!

When any man or woman is called to a special task in the service of the Lord they are given the enabling through the precious gift of the Holy Spirit in their lives. Thus it is his power not our human strength or wisdom that accomplishes his will, and only he gets the glory. This cannot be over-emphasized. To lose sight of this basic spiritual truth is to open the door to division within the body of Christ. There can surely be no greater sin than to allow our human pride and self-glorification to bring division and suffering upon the body of our Lord. When his people, who are his body, are torn asunder, he is torn apart. He suffers a fresh crucifixion. Our sins are the nails that pierce him and our loveless lives are the hands that drive them into him.

In response to the urgency of the times God is blowing the trumpet worldwide, calling his people in every nation into action. There are approximately one thousand million people in the world today who claim to be Christian. They are drawn from almost every nation and community in the world. Many of them are nominal in their faith and commitment, but the call is still addressed to them. God is calling all who claim the name of Jesus to a fresh commitment and obedience to him. He is calling them to listen to his word and to heed the warnings that he is sending to the world. In our generation he is giving a fresh outpouring of the Holy Spirit to all peoples in fulfilment of the promise he made through his servant Joel and according to the vision seen by Peter on the day of Pentecost when the new age was inaugurated – the 'age of grace' through the in-dwelling power of the Holy Spirit with the people of God who accept Jesus as Saviour and Lord (Joel 2:28, Acts 2:17).

Today God is raising a people of power. They are a prophetic people. They are given the ability to discern the signs of the times. They are both men and women who are given the spiritual gifts to carry out the task to which God is calling them among the nations. The Gideon's army of today is a Spirit-filled company of men and women who know the power of God in their own lives and who are prepared to be living witnesses to their own generation. They have a heightened spiritual awareness because of a special anointing of the Holy Spirit. The task God is laying upon them is not one of world leadership, but of world witness!

From among the millions of men and women throughout the nations who belong to him through Christ God is calling together a great army of volunteers. It is from among them

– those who are responsive to his will and who heed his call – that God is calling out his Gideon's army for special service. As with the original three hundred, they are only a small company among the multitudes of his people.

Like the original band who with Gideon crept down the hillside through the night to face the enemy and what humanly speaking was an impossible task, the people who form Gideon's army of today are a tiny minority of utterly dedicated Spirit-filled Christians who bear all the same characteristics of Gideon's original band. They are courageous in the face of the enemy and persevere even in times of difficulty and discouragement. They have a spirit of discernment and are ever alert and watchful for the moves of the enemy, but they do not keep their eyes on the enemy and allow him to dictate their moves. Their eyes are upon the Lord, for they know that the battle is his and the outcome is assured.

They are men and women who have the gift of faith. They have what Paul would call a special measure of faith above the ordinary measure of faith that enables them to have absolute trust in the Lord. Their faith also enables them to be obedient, to give absolute obedience to the Lord. When he speaks they obey without question. They are men and women of vision who have glimpsed something of the overall purposes of God through the gift of the spirit of wisdom that gives them insight into the heavenly realms beyond our human understanding. They are men and women who are prepared and trained and who know that spiritual training is never completed. It requires daily waiting upon the Lord and spiritual exercises that continually heighten our receptivity to the word of the Lord. They are men and women who are utterly disciplined and who know how to exercise self-control in the power of the Spirit.

These are the characteristics of the twentieth-century Gideon's army that God is raising, the people of power that he is calling together from among the nations of the world. Many will volunteer for service but few will be chosen, as Jesus himself said. But this does not mean that all the volunteers who are responsive to his will are rejected by God; far from it! Every one is loved and needed and each one has a place in the overall purposes of God. He has good plans for each one of his children, plans for good and not for evil to give us a future and a hope. His strategy and his timing are perfect. He is making them known to some of his servants to whom he has given the special ministry of the prophet in this generation.

The company of the prophets is a small band of people drawn from among many nations who are seeing the purposes of God revealed to them. At the moment they do not know each other, and many are exercising lonely ministries, but the day will come when they will be in communication with each other because God is calling together a company of the prophets to serve him within their own nations and cultures, that all his people may hear his prophetic word for today in their own tongues and within their own understanding.

The task of this contemporary Gideon's army is to respond to that prophetic word, to catch the vision as it is revealed and to form a disciplined, trained, obedient and courageous army of Spirit-filled men and women of faith and discernment to spearhead the assault upon the enemy strongholds.

The members of Gideon's army today will know of their calling through the witness of the Spirit within them. The Spirit will also bear witness to other members of the body of Christ within their own communities and there will be confirming signs within their lives. The first sign is their willing response to the word of the Lord which brings them into the larger army of his volunteers. From among them the Spirit-filled special service unit is being formed for the task that lies ahead. None must go ahead of the timing of the Lord. Each must be disciplined in watching and praying and waiting upon the Lord.

The day is at hand when the denizens of the night will be uncovered and the purposes of God will be revealed to the children of light. Many are already aware of what is happening in our world today. God is not a God of confusion, but of order. He does not speak a word to one of his servants and then a contradictory word to another. He confirms his word in the mouths of the prophets. There is a unity and harmony in the revelation of God even though the expression of the vision is different. To those with eyes to see and ears to hear the word of the Lord is plain to discern. The signs of the times are clear. We are moving towards the end of this age.

The increasing turmoil in the world, within communities and between the nations, as nation rises against nation, will cause people of all nations to tremble with fear and foreboding. This will prepare the way for the witness of God's modern Gideon's army through whom he will make his appeal to the peoples of the world. Their prophetic witness will be a word of warning, a call to repentance and an offer of hope. The prophetic word of the Lord does not change from one generation to another. It is still the same as the word God spoke to ancient Israel:

'Come now, let us reason together', says the Lord. 'Though your sins are like scarlet, they shall be as white as snow; though they are as red as crimson, they shall be like wool. If you are willing and obedient, you will eat the best from the land; but if you resist and rebel, you will be devoured by the sword.' For the mouth of the Lord has spoken. (Isaiah 1:8–20)

That same choice is still open to the nations of the world. It is not too late to hear and heed the word of the Lord and to turn to him and be saved. It is not too late for the nations to stop in their tracks, in the very path that leads to destruction. God is pleading with the nations today to turn to him and be saved from the forces of destruction that are gathering upon the horizon like the dark clouds of a mighty storm. Soon that storm will be let loose and will begin to sweep across the world like a mighty hurricane with unstoppable fury, tearing asunder the civilization of the centuries.

God is warning the nations today of the inevitability of the death and destruction that is coming if they continue to tread their present path. But God is saying there is still an 'unless': 'It will happen *unless* you repent and turn to me for I alone can turn back the forces of destruction that will surely overwhelm you. You cannot save yourselves. You cannot face the enemy behind the storm clouds of death in your own strength. Turn to me and be saved. I love you. You are my children. I made you in my own image. I made my world and saw that it was good. I do not wish to see my children suffer and the whole creation groan under the weight of sorrow and destruction.'

The task of Gideon's army is to convey the pleading of God to his world. Theirs is the task of bearing the Father's heart to his children. The ground is being prepared. The day is coming soon when they will witness to the world. The army is already being called together. The people of power are being prepared. The day when they will face the enemy is soon to dawn. The trumpet will sound among the nations!

CHAPTER EIGHT

The Signs of the Times

God is breaking his heart over his world. If we can grieve over our children, when we see them making terrible blunders and they refuse to accept our guidance, how much greater is God's sorrow over us. He knows what lies ahead on the path being taken by the nations and he is urgently calling, 'Turn to me and be saved, all you ends of the earth, for I am God and there is no other' (Isaiah 45:22).

He is longing to embrace all mankind in his fatherly love and he is weeping over the nations today as Jesus wept over the city of Jerusalem shortly before its people rejected and crucified him. 'As he approached Jerusalem and saw the city, he wept over it and said, "If you, even you, had only known on this day what would bring you peace – but now it is hidden from your eyes"' (Luke 19:41–42).

God is urgently warning us of the dangers we are facing, while at the same time he is reminding us of his great love for us and of his loving good purposes.

It is God's intention to break the powers of evil that are driving mankind. He will one day overcome the principalities and powers that have taken control of the nations and are at present impelling them headlong towards destruction. It is God's intention to overcome the strongholds of spiritual wickedness and to establish his own authority over the whole created order. He cannot for ever tolerate the dominion of the enemy over man, whom he loves. He has declared:

It is I who made the earth and created mankind upon it. My own hands stretched out the heavens; I marshalled their starry hosts. (Isaiah 45:12)

God is carefully watching the rapidly changing scene on earth. He is deeply concerned for his people. The day will come when 'all who have raged against him will come to him and be put to shame' (Isaiah 45:24).

Through the Cross God has already given notice to the enemy. He has opened the way of salvation to all believers. He has made it possible for each individual to enter into a right relationship with himself, freely forgiven and cleansed from sin: 'In the Lord all the descendants of Israel will be found righteous and will exult.' The true descendants of Israel are not the descendants of the flesh but the descendants of the Spirit. It is those who are redeemed by Christ who are the inheritors of the covenant and the promises.

Many Christians find it difficult to understand the enigma of the sovereign love of God and the presence of evil in the world. If God is Lord of lords and King of kings, if he is the God of all creation who created all things and put them under his dominion, why is man still driven by the forces of evil? The answer is much more simple than the theologians sometimes make it appear. Quite simply, the battle against the arch-enemy has yet to take place. Through the Cross God has made it possible for each individual to break free from the grip of the enemy and to come into a right relationship with himself. God has created man in his own image, but he has also given to him freedom of will. This offers him the choice: either he can come into the fullness of a love relationship with the Father through the Son or he can reject his love and remain outside that love relationship. So long as men on earth remain outside that love relationship which is characteristic of God's kingdom and of life within his family, they are open to the enemy, driven by the forces of evil that lead to destruction and death.

God will not allow man to destroy the earth. It is his creation, the work of his hands:

God saw all that he had made, and it was very good.
(Genesis 1:31)

Jesus tells us that God loves his world. He didn't say that God simply loves the men and women whom he has created in his own image but that 'God so loved the *world* that he gave his one and only Son' (John 3:16).

But due to the immense powers of destruction now in the hands of man the danger facing the world is so great as to threaten the future existence of life on this planet.

There is a growing urgency in the action God is taking. He is, in fact, doing four things of which Christians need to be aware.

A MESSAGE OF LOVE

God is reminding us of his love. In a time of increasing world turmoil the first requirement for Christians is to come to a fresh understanding and experience of the centrality of the love of God. We cannot understand God's great and good purposes for mankind if we do not begin with his love. The love of God was the focal point of the message and ministry of Jesus. He continually spoke of the fatherhood of God and taught his hearers to understand the nature of that fatherly love.

Christians need to turn again to John's gospel for an understanding of the fatherhood of God. The central point of that understanding is to be found in John 3:16 and 17.

For God so loved the world that he gave his one and only Son, that whoever believes in him shall not perish but have eternal life. For God did not send his Son into the world to condemn the world, but to save the world through him.

Jesus's teaching was that God loves the world – that means the whole created order that he formed with his own hands and made so incredibly beautiful. For the sake of his children, men and women whom he made in his own spiritual image, he gave his one and only Son so that they could have eternal life with him, enjoying the blessings of his presence and abiding in his love for ever. In sending the Son it was not God's purpose to condemn the world. But mevitably those who do not respond to the great and good purposes of God when they are clearly communicated to them condemn themselves and put themselves outside the life-giving relationship of God's fatherly love.

It was God's purpose to save the world through Jesus and

Whoever believes in him is not condemned, but whoever does not believe stands condemned already because he has not believed in the name of God's one and only Son.

(John 3:18)

Through Jesus God presents mankind with a clear choice, and yet it is not the choice of threat but the choice of love. Either we choose love and enter into life with all its joys and blessings, or we are driven by hate and violence and the forces of destruction that lead to death.

God is reminding us today of the centrality of his love for four reasons.

Firstly, it is not his will that destruction should come upon mankind. He longs to be in a loving fatherly relationship with all his children and it is not his will that one should perish.

Secondly, if the nations of the world will hear the word of God and repent, destruction will not come upon them. The message of Jonah is relevant for our times. God offered the people of Nineveh the choice of life or death. Repentance meant life; refusal to hear his word spelt death. The people of that great city chose life and repented when they heard the message. That same choice is ours today, as God has made clear through Jeremiah.

If at any time I announce that a nation or kingdom is to be uprooted, torn down and destroyed, and if that nation I warned repents of its evil, then I will relent and not inflict on it the disaster I had planned.   (Jeremiah 18:7 and 8)

Thirdly, God works in the world to bring his word through

his people. This is why God is reminding his people of his love – so that they will understand his ways, his fatherly care, his great and good purposes for the whole family of mankind. He wants to convey this message to the world through all his people; for this reason he wishes his love to be seen within the Church and thus revealed to all mankind.

The fourth reason why God is reminding us of his love today is that he does not wish his people to be afraid in these days of increasing turmoil. As the increasing violence of man disturbs every community, fear will grip men's hearts. God wants his people to be unafraid; he is reassuring them of his fatherly love and care. Their salvation is guaranteed. They are citizens of another city whose architect and builder is God. 'Fear not, little flock', Jesus said to his own disciples and he is bringing a similar message to all his people today:

> Do not let your hearts be troubled. Trust in God, trust also in me.   (John 14:1)

God is grieving over his world as it rushes towards destruction. He is grieving over his own people, so unaware of what is happening in the world. He is grieving over their lack of vision and their lack of trust in him. God wants all his people to be a prophetic people, witnessing to the world today. Through those who are committed to him in Christ Jesus he wants to bring the Gospel of salvation to all mankind.

'Tell my people I love them', he is saying. But the Christians themselves have first to hear the message and to understand it. We only understand the minutest part of the love of God for us. We Christians need to be rooted and grounded in the love of God that we 'may have power, together with all the saints, to grasp how wide and long and high and deep is the love of Christ, and to know this love that surpasses knowledge' (Ephesians 3:18 and 19). When we Christians show the love of God to the world, then his message will be heard.

A MESSAGE OF WARNING

In addition to reminding us of his love, God is also sending us a message of warning. He knows that the untamed fury of man will tear his world apart. A small child in a temper-tantrum is good evidence of this. If an infant had the power of a man he would destroy everything around him. Immature men in an age of violence are a menace to the whole of mankind. The untamed nature of man, into whose hands are placed the ultimate weapons of physical destruction, will destroy the world. The diminishing natural resources of the world such as oil and other basic minerals needed for the ever-expanding industrial plant of the world's rapidly growing cities will one day cause greedy unredeemed men to risk the ultimate consequences of the ultimate conflict.

Even secular politicians are becoming worried about the increasing threat of war. It is not only the youth of today in the cities of the Western world who are worried. They demonstrate against policies of their governments that they know will eventually lead to international madness and the nuclear holocaust. Every sane observer of the international scene is aware of the immense danger facing mankind. But what no man can know, unless God reveals it to him, is that there is no force on earth that can stop the forces of evil except the power of God, because man is being driven by the ancient enemy of mankind. There is no way we can resist him except by a greater spiritual power. Secular man does not understand the nature of the war in which he is involved. He can only think in terms of political strategies. He does not understand spiritual warfare and the danger is increased because the enemy convinces us that we can win in our own strength.

Paul certainly understood spiritual warfare. He vividly describes the struggle he experienced in his religious life before the encounter with Christ. He says:

> For what I do is not the good I want to do; no, the evil I do not want to do – this I keep on doing.   (Romans 7:19)

Paul was conscious of the presence of another power within him that appeared to take control of his actions. It seemed to override his will. It was an external force. He did not find any power within himself with which to come against this external force. Whenever he tried to combat it in order to fulfil the requirements of the law he failed. Paul really understood and appreciated the rightness and justice of the requirements of the law. For him the law was beautiful and holy. With his mind he 'delighted in the law'. For Paul, the central tragedy was that 'the law is spiritual; but I am unspiritual, sold as a slave to sin' (Romans 7:14).

Paul summed up the struggle that he experienced in his personal life in a classic statement of the nature of spiritual warfare.

> So I find this law at work: when I want to do good, evil is right there with me. For in my inner being I delight in God's law; but I see another law at work in the members of my body, waging war against the law of my mind and making me a prisoner of the law of sin at work within my members. (Romans 7:21–23)

Paul then uses a powerful figure of speech. He says, 'What a wretched man I am!' and then demands, 'Who will rescue me from this body of death?' He no doubt had in mind a vivid picture of the Roman judicial system which required the punishment to fit the crime. In some provinces of the Roman empire magistrates would order a convicted murderer to bear the body of his victim. For certain types of murder it was the practice to take the body of the murdered man and strap it on to the back of the murderer with bronze or iron fetters that could not be removed. Everywhere the murderer went he would carry the body of his victim. No one would help him remove it. It was a permanent burden on his back, a constant witness against him that he was a man of violence, a convicted felon. Moreover the corpse of the murdered man gradually rotted. The stench became intolerable. Disease from the decaying flesh on his back was communicated to the

113

body of the murderer and eventually he died by the hand of the man whom he had murdered. Justice was done; Roman justice!

Paul carried in his mind the unforgettable sight of a man, back bent under the strain of that fearful burden, that hulk of rotting flesh strapped to his back that he could not remove and which no one would take away from him. He knew that eventually the body on his back would kill him. Paul identified with the convicted man who bore that burden. He saw himself struggling to free himself from that hulk of contagious corruption that clung so closely to him and spelt inevitable death.

'Who will rescue me from this body of death?' he cried. And then came the answer and the triumphal shout of victory – only Jesus Christ can do this. He not only can do it, he has *done* it!

Thanks be to God – through Jesus Christ our Lord!

(v. 25)

For Paul there was only one answer to spiritual warfare and that was to let God take over the battle. Through Jesus the Holy Spirit was available to man and he alone had power to overcome the enemy.

Through Christ Jesus the law of the spirit of life set me free from the law of sin and death. (Romans 8:2)

Paul realized that there are some things that man cannot do for himself. There are limits imposed by our humanity that spell death if we ignore them when battling in the spiritual realm. This is a battle in which we need God's help. He warned the Christians in Ephesus to

Put on the full armour of God so that you can take your stand against the devil's schemes. For our struggle is not against flesh and blood, but against the rulers, against the authorities, against the powers of this dark world and

against the spiritual forces of evil in the heavenly realms.
(Ephesians 6:11–12)

Paul's words of warning apply not only to us as individuals in our personal battle against sin; they apply to whole communities and to nations. Strapped to the back of the nations is the body of death imposed by the enemy of mankind. That rotting, decaying corpse is transmitting its corruption at an ever-increasing rate into the disease-ridden, famine-stricken, suffering body of mankind. The nations are struggling ever more violently to shake off the body of death that is gradually sucking the life and health from the body of mankind. But men are powerless to break the fetters. Only God can do that! And he is offering that power to us today.

God has given us the way of salvation, the way of love, through the Cross of Jesus that has opened up the way to life for every believer. He is today offering the way of life to the nations. It is the only alternative to the way of death: repentance, turning to him and seeking his way. Through trust in God, through the ways of righteousness and peace there will flow through the life of the nations a spiritual antibiotic powerful enough to overcome the corrupting forces of death that are driving mankind to inevitable destruction. Only his love can overcome the violence of the enemy.

AN OUTPOURING OF THE SPIRIT

God is sending an overflowing of his love to his people today to arm them for the battle. The power to overcome the enemy and to confound his plans is available to man through the Holy Spirit. It is, perhaps, only in our day that we are beginning to see the full significance of Pentecost. On that day God gave his precious gift of the Holy Spirit to the believers in Christ. The power of the Spirit was made available to all who accepted Jesus as Lord and Saviour. Previously the Spirit had only been given to certain anointed individuals, chosen leaders, men set aside for specific tasks of leadership in the life of the old Israel. Now in the new

Israel, at Pentecost, the Spirit was given to all believers, the whole community of Christ had the power to become a discerning, prophetic people to witness to the world and to carry out the purposes of God that were begun in Christ Jesus.

The Holy Spirit enables us to understand the purposes of God and to discern the way he is guiding us. The Holy Spirit also enables us to communicate with God and to hear what he is saying to us. It is of the greatest significance that the Spirit enables God's people to discern that which is of his Spirit and that which is not. It guarantees the authenticity of the word of God. It guards the body of Christ against error. It guarantees the people of the Lord against being misled by false prophecies, by the wiles of the enemy or even by the antics of the anti-Christ.

A further reason for the fresh movement of the Holy Spirit we are seeing today is that God is longing to draw millions of his children to him. In nations previously unevangelized there is real evidence of a spiritual awakening as the Gospel reaches many communities who had previously never heard of Jesus Christ. Church growth experts tell us that Africa, south of the Sahara, is rapidly becoming the new Christian spiritual centre of the world. More than six million Africans are being added to the Lord every year and the new-birth rate now exceeds the natural-birth rate. Thus the day is in sight when the whole of Africa will be evangelized and the vast majority will become committed Christians. There is similar evidence from many other parts of the world including Asia, where in many countries such as Korea large numbers are committing their lives to Christ in a nation where just one generation ago there were only a handful of Christians. We do not yet know the full story of what God is doing in China but the picture that is emerging encourages us to believe that the Church is growing rapidly among that nation's vast multitudes.

It is the *rate* of growth that is causing the greatest excitement among Christians. The Church today is growing at a faster rate than ever before since the first century. The day is actually in sight when the whole world will be evangelized. It is estimated that by the year AD 2000 ninety-three per cent of the world's population will have been reached with the Gospel, will have had the opportunity of hearing the Gospel for themselves, in their own language, brought to their own communities, even if they do not all become committed Christians.

One of the signs of the end of the age that Jesus gave in the list that Matthew records in chapter twenty-four is that:

> This gospel of the kingdom will be preached in the whole world as a testimony to all the nations.   (v. 14)

Jesus clearly did not envisage everyone in the world receiving him as Lord and Saviour. But he did declare that before the end of the age everyone would have the opportunity of hearing the witness of the Gospel. That day is now in sight.

God is also longing to renew his Church with power to meet the demands of this day. In many lands where there has been a Christian presence for centuries there is evidence of a movement of spiritual renewal. In South America, where millions have been nominal Christians for generations, there is a fresh outpouring of the Holy Spirit that is bringing whole communities alive in Christ. It is not an exaggeration to say that millions have been filled with the Holy Spirit during the past one or two decades. This new movement of the Spirit is transforming the scene in nation after nation on the South American continent.

In the Western world, similarly, there is evidence of a fresh movement of the Spirit. In Europe, where the Church has become highly institutionalized over the centuries, with the result that it has been powerless to resist the onslaught of secularism during the past hundred years, the renewing power of the Holy Spirit is now solidly in evidence. In Britain the renewal movement has not been confined to the growth of independent charismatic fellowships but has been making steady inroads into the major branches of the traditional Church, including the Anglicans and the Roman Catholics. Tens of thousands meet regularly in inter-denominational prayer fellowships where the gifts of the Holy Spirit are exercised. In most towns and cities throughout the country there are regular celebrations for prayer, praise and healing that include some exposition of the word of God. There are strong indications that the renewal movement in Britain may soon overflow into full-scale revival in the life of the nation. This has already happened in Finland where revival has been taking place since the late 1970s.

Throughout the Western world, in major nations such as America, Canada, Australia as well as in the old countries of Europe, there is overwhelming evidence of a new movement of the Holy Spirit. This is bringing fresh life and enthusiasm to Christians and a new spiritual impetus to the work of evangelism and service in the world. It is resulting in a steady growth of the Church in most countries, but above all it is raising the expectations of Christians. It is when there is a real expectancy and the people of God wait upon him in prayer that mighty things begin to happen. There is a new emphasis upon intercession, a fresh understanding of the purposes of God that is bringing vision and hope to his people. It is bringing also a new sense of urgency to their witness in the world. God is re-arming his people with the power and might of his Spirit.

THE ARMY OF THE LORD

It is in response to the immense dangers facing mankind that God is raising a vast army throughout the world, filled with the power of his Spirit. It is an army of volunteers. It is an international army drawn from every nation, every culture and every community. There are no bounds and no boundaries. The army of the Lord is not a part-time rabble but a full-time company of utterly dedicated men, women and young people who have responded to the call of their Creator, who have received Jesus as Lord in their lives and the power of the Holy Spirit has come upon them.

The army of the Lord is a worldwide army. It is composed of all those who have responded to the trumpet call that God is sending out to all his people today. Among those who have responded to his call, God is calling together a smaller task force, a special service unit, a Gideon's army. They are men and women of all ages who are aware of the special dangers facing mankind. They have the spirit of discernment that enables them to perceive the actions of the enemy and the strategies being employed to encompass the destruction of mankind. They are also able to discern the direction that the Holy Spirit is taking in leading his people to counter the moves of the enemy.

We began this book with the incident on the mountainside at Adelboden in Switzerland, where a small child was sliding down the snowcovered slope towards the edge of the precipice and certain death. Her father responded immediately to the cry of his child and rushed to her aid, snatching her from the very jaws of death. But what would have happened if that child had not cried out? Her father would not even have been aware of her plight. She could have slid silently down to her death. But God has implanted in each of us an instinctive awareness of danger, a fear that makes us cry out for help when we experience the feeling of helplessness in the face of immense danger. The little girl cried out with the full power of her lungs, and with her eyes she looked up imploringly to her father. He responded at once. His love overcame his own fear as he hurled himself down the mountainside. Love overcame fear. He saved his child. That is how God loves us and responds to our cries for help. In giving a fresh outpouring of the Holy Spirit today God is giving gifts to his people. He is heightening the awareness of danger in many of those who have responded to his call. They are being driven to prayer by a deepening sense of burden for our world, for our nations, for our communities, for mankind. They are becoming God's army of prayer warriors. They are the intercessors for the world who are waiting upon God daily in a mighty prayer chain that is encircling the world and lifting the nations before the Father at such a time as this.

From the vast army of his people worldwide God is calling together a smaller, Spirit-filled army, disciplined, trained and ready to face the enemy, able to discern the nature of the battle, obedient and trusting, not running ahead but waiting upon the Lord and waiting for his timing. They have a special task to witness not only to the world but to their brothers and sisters in the Lord. Theirs is the task to discern the relevant word of God for today and to witness within the body of Christ. It is the basic prophetic task that was carried out by the ancient prophets of Israel in days of danger when God spoke directly to those whom he had anointed for the task. Just as in ancient Israel, whenever God sent a prophetic warning to his people he both showed them the inevitability of destruction if they continued to pursue the course upon which they were set and he also held out new life and hope if they turned from their wicked ways, so God is offering the same choice today. It is a choice that is being offered to all the nations of the world. It is the choice between life and death.

God loves his world and is calling upon the nations to turn to him and be saved. He is giving a fresh understanding of his love to his own people so that they may witness to the world of the great saving purposes of God. His plans are for good and not for evil, to give the whole of mankind a future and a hope. He is making these plans known through his modern Gideon's army, but he wants all his people to be a prophetic people. The day will come when the whole army of God is mobilized and brought into action to witness to a dying world.

Now is the time for Christians to open their eyes to what God is doing in his world and to enter into the victory he has already won in Jesus. It is our privilege to share in the power he is making available to us through the Holy Spirit as the battle ground is being prepared for the final conflict with the enemy of mankind. The victory is assured, for his is the kingdom, the power and the glory, for ever and ever.

Hallelujah! Our God reigns!

Practical Guidelines for Christians

Being and Doing

I am constantly being asked by Christians what we should be doing to meet the demands of the times in which we live. There are no easy answers to this and every Christian will need to seek God for specific guidance for his or her own situation. There is no blueprint that applies to all Christians everywhere. I do believe, however, that our God is faithful in guiding his people if we are faithful in waiting upon him. We need to be a *listening* people as well as an action-oriented one.

God always answers prayer – specific, directed, believing prayer. We need to have the discernment to perceive the answer, the faith to respond correctly, the trust to go forward confidently and the power of the Holy Spirit to walk in his strength and in his ways.

The following are a few simple guidelines to help in praying through your response to this book.

1. BEING

(a) *Commitment.* Remember, the army of the Lord is an army of volunteers! Gideon's army of three hundred was a special service unit called together for the special task of spearheading the action. The whole army of the Lord was 32,000 strong. They were those who had responded when the trumpet call went out through the land sounding the alarm and the call to action.

Hence the first requirement of every Christian today is

positive response, total commitment. You don't need to sign any enlistment papers, but you do need to tell the Lord very clearly and positively that you are totally committing your life to him. Even if you've said it before; say it again *now* as a deliberate act of commitment to whatever *new things* God has to show to you.

(*b*) *Lifestyle*. Pray about your lifestyle. God wants his people to BE as well as to DO! How should a Christian live in these days? There ought to be a difference in the lifestyle of Christians. Can your friends and neighbours (or non-Christian relatives) *see* a difference between your lifestyle and that of non-Christians? Don't just guess at the answer – ask them! Then; don't argue with the answers you are given by them, take them before the Lord in prayer. He will show you whether or not the judgement of your non-Christian friends is just or unjust. He will also show you what to do about it. If you do not know any non-Christians you can ask – make that an urgent matter of repentance! Remember that the purpose of an army is to combat the enemy not to live in a cosy protected garrison leaving others to fight the war.

(*c*) *Witness*. Being a witness involves both being and doing. Hence we have included the heading 'witness' under both sections. It is essential to remember that we are witnessing all the time whether we wish to or not. As a committed Christian whenever we are with others we are never 'off-duty' even though we may be relaxing in the company of other Christians. We are still making a witness by our words, by our deeds, by our attitudes and by the unspoken communication of our beliefs, values, faith and trust, through our being – our 'body language' and spiritual encounter.

When we are with non-Christians we are never 'off-duty' from the obligation to accept opportunities to make a specific witness when the occasion arises. If we are known to be Christians we are inevitably making a witness of some kind, even if we are not conscious of doing so.

The New Testament term for a Christian was a witness. We are all witnesses. We are either a good witness or a bad witness.

(d) Love. God wants his people to be a loving people. 'My command is this', said Jesus. 'Love each other as I have loved you' (John 15:12). How did Jesus love me? – he gave himself for me. That is how I must love others; without reserve, not putting myself and my own self-interest first.

There needs to be a special love among Christians within each local fellowship. We need almost to be surpassing each other in love. Love binds the body together and creates unity and strength. Love is the most neglected gift in the Church today, yet it is the greatest because it is nearest to the nature and the very essence of God. Without love we are nothing. We certainly do not and cannot reflect the face of God in the world. 'If I have not love, I am only a resounding gong or a clanging cymbal . . . If I give all I possess to the poor and surrender my body to the flames, but have not love I gain nothing' (1 Corinthians 13:1–3).

How can we love non-Christians if we do not even love Christians? How can we speak to our neighbours of love if there is no love in our own family? How can we respond to God's call to 'Tell my people I love them' if we do not love one another? How can we say we love God whom we have not seen when we do not love those whom we see daily? 'If anyone says, "I love God" yet hates his brother, he is a liar. For anyone who does not love his brother whom he has seen, cannot love God whom he has not seen' (1 John 4:20).

2. DOING

(a) Study. We cannot make a prophetic witness if we do not understand the message or the situation into which the message is directed. This requires study. Our study needs to have two thrusts: into the world, and towards God.

We need to be aware of what is happening around us in our local community, town and nation and among the nations of the world. This means keeping broadly abreast of the news. We need to know what is happening in the world if we are to convey God's word to people today. It's a good idea to supplement the daily news with a good magazine that collects information from around the world which rarely appears in the press, such as *The New Internationalist*, a monthly magazine produced by a group of Christians concerned with world issues such as poverty, hunger and disease.

Of course, it should not need to be said that we also need to study the Bible. There is no substitute for in-depth study of the word of God to discover what he is saying to his world today.

In addition to regular systematic study of scripture, we need to take the current issues in the news to the Bible to see what God has said concerning such things in the past. Our study of scripture should not only lead us into a closer walk with God but to a better knowledge of his ways and understanding of his overall purposes for mankind.

(b) Prayer. There is no substitute for prayer. We need regular communion with God. Prayer includes listening, being quiet before the Lord, as well as talking. 'Be still and know that I am God' (Psalm 46:10). 'In quietness and trust shall be your strength' (Isaiah 30:15).

Prayer also includes intercession. This means work. Waiting upon God in intercessory prayer is hard, demanding work. It requires concentration, determination and perseverance. It needs the kind of persistence urged by the prophet who longed to see Jerusalem rebuilt. 'You who call upon the Lord, give yourselves no rest, and give him no rest until he establishes Jerusalem and makes her the praise of the earth' (Isaiah 62:6–7). Jesus also urged perseverance in prayer in his parable of the persistent widow (Luke 18:1–8).

Prayer is not simply saying words. It is entering into the presence of the Almighty and communicating with him through praise, adoration, confession, thanksgiving, petition, plus specific, directed, believing intercession and through quiet, patient, expectant listening.

(c) *Witness*. It is not easy to give guidelines on witness as each of us is different. Each Christian has a unique combination of gifts, and therefore we each need to express our faith in ways that uniquely suit our personalities as well as our circumstances (which also are unique to us). God wants his people today to be a prophetic witness in the world. Remember that the primary task of the prophet has always been to forthtell the word of God; to tell others what God has said to him. That is precisely what God wants from his people today. He wants us to be a listening and a responsive people, obedient to him and trusting his word. Our witness is to tell others what God is saying to his people today and through them to his world. That is being a prophetic people.

To be an active witness means to be involved practically in sharing our faith and in self-sacrificial service – not only among Christians, but also within secular society – in our local community and wherever possible in the wider world. Evangelism and service are not two optional alternatives for Christians. They are both imperatives.

(d) *Small Groups*. Every Christian should belong to a small group of committed Christians where all the above three activities can be pursued. This is in addition to individual action. We need each other. We need to study scripture together, to exercise the gifts within the body, to seek the Lord together through study of his word and, through discussion of what is happening in the world around us.

Have a regular programme. It is a good idea, in addition to Bible study, to take a book such as my *The Day Comes* and work through it, especially studying the Bible references in relation to the signs of the times. We also need corporate prayer. It is through waiting upon the Lord together that the gifts, especially the gift of prophecy, can be rightly exercised. But study carefully Paul's warnings in 1 Corinthians 14 and 1 Thessalonians 5; also see 1 John 4. Our corporate prayer life should not only deepen our walk with God and our understanding of his word but should give us a clear direction for action through corporate witness. Ask for specific guidance for your group and your church, for what you should be doing to convey his word to the community around you, through evangelism and through service.

(e) *Love*. None of our witness or action in the world will be effective without love. But love is not a trifling emotion. It is a powerful sentiment that drives us into action. The essence of love is identification with others. This is the heart of both the incarnation of Jesus and the Cross. 'He made himself nothing, taking the very nature of a servant, being made in human likeness. And being found in appearance as a man, he humbled himself and became obedient to death – even to death on a Cross!' (Philippians 2:7 and 8). 'He was pierced for our transgressions, he was crushed for our iniquities' (Isaiah 53:5).

Christians need to enter into the experience of suffering in our sin-stricken world. It is not enough to express horror and indignation at the injustices suffered by others, or at the violence and hatred seen in our world. We need to feel the sinfulness *as though it were our own*, as though we had committed the crime. We need to identify with the victims of oppression, injustice and violence as though we stood in their place. Then we shall feel the burden of the world.

Then we shall enter into the experience of Isaiah: 'I am a man of unclean lips and I live among a people of unclean lips' (Isaiah 6:5). Then we shall be driven to go to God with the burden of our generation, of our community, our nation and our world. That is the basis of true intercession – carrying a love burden to the Lord, as when a mother cries out to God for her wayward child, or a father comes before the Lord breaking his heart for his rebellious son. The parents cry before God as though the sins of their children were their own sins. That is a love burden. That is when you begin to enter into the fellowship of Christ's sufferings. That is when your intercession changes from mere words into loving, dynamic prayer. That is love in action.

There is another side of love in action, and that is its practical expression in the world. It is easy to love those who love us. It is easy to love the lovely. But it is not easy to love those who would be our enemies. It is not easy to love the unlovely. But that is what love is all about. 'God demonstrates his own love for us in this; while we were still sinners Christ died for us' (Romans 5:8).

Jesus says that the practical expression of our love for him is in our love for others. Read Matthew 25:31–46: 'Whatever you did for the least of these brothers of mine, you did for me.' Who were these brothers of Jesus? – they were the hungry, the stranger, the sick and the prisoner! God is saying, 'Tell My People I Love Them' – but tell them in words that are clothed in deeds.

Finally our love witness needs to be prophetic. God is calling his people today to tell the world that the nations are treading the path leading to destruction. This is not his will for mankind. God is calling the nations to repentance. Every Christian has the duty to share in this prophetic task to make the word of God known, to tell the world of the love of God and of his saving purposes.

'Tell my people I love them' means 'Tell all men everywhere'. Proclaim it from the housetops. God is love! His ways are the ways of peace and life and love for all mankind.

God is saying to us today:

TELL MY PEOPLE I LOVE THEM!

TELL MY PEOPLE I LOVE THEM
TELL MY PEOPLE I CARE.
WHEN THEY FEEL FAR AWAY FROM ME
TELL MY PEOPLE I'M THERE.